POWERPOINT
MADE EASY

Presenting Your Ideas With Style

By James Bernstein

Bernstein, James
PowerPoint Made Easy
Book 12 in the Computers Made Easy series

For more information on reproducing sections of this book or sales of this book,
go to **www.madeeasybookseries.com**

Contents

Introduction

Microsoft PowerPoint has been around for many years and is the go to program when it comes to creating professional looking presentations that can be used for a variety of purposes from making a slide show for your kid's classroom project or presenting your big sales pitch at the corporate meeting.

Creating basic presentations is fairly simple and that's one of the things that makes PowerPoint such a great tool to use to get your point across to just about any audience. Of course it takes a little know how to add some flair to your presentation to really wow your audience and even that is not too difficult once you get the hang of how things work.

The goal of this book is to teach you how to get up and running with PowerPoint and show you how all the tools and menu options work, so you know where you need to go to do what you need to do. I will go over how to create basic presentations as well as how to add some advanced features to them so you can make yourself look like a pro even if you might not be!

I will be using PowerPoint 2019 for my examples but if you are using any version from PowerPoint 2010 and up (maybe even 2007) then it should be fairly easy to follow along since things have not really changed that much in regards to where you go to find the tools needed to get things done.

What this book is not, is a book on advanced PowerPoint even though I will be going into some of the more advanced features of the software. Now that I think about it, I don't know if there is even anything too advanced about PowerPoint that real people like us would even use in the first place.

So on that note, let's get started making some eye catching presentations that will be sure to wow your audience... and maybe even yourself!

Chapter 1 – What is PowerPoint?

If you are reading this book you most likely have an idea of what Microsoft PowerPoint is used for or even have used it yourself to create your own presentations. These presentations are kind of like slideshows with information such as text, charts, pictures, etc. rather than just a photo slideshow that you might be more used to seeing.

These presentations are used to "present" your information to your audience to educate or enlighten them on the particular subject you wish to have them learn more about. This is done using multiple slides to convey your information sort of like pages in a manual with each slide containing whatever text or media you wish to display.

You can then have the slides tie together with transitions and animations to give your presentation a more complete feel and keep your audience entertained (and awake!) at the same time. Then once you have all your slides configured the way you like, you simply have them shown as "a show" and can use the mouse or keyboard to click your way between the slides and any custom transitions you created. (Animations and transitions will be covered in Chapter 5).

PowerPoint Interface
The PowerPoint interface (figure 1.1) is pretty simple and consists of the main work area where you will add things such as text, pictures, charts, videos and so on. Then on the left of the screen, you will see your individual slides (often called the slide deck), and this is where you can click on a specific slide to work on that slide's content.

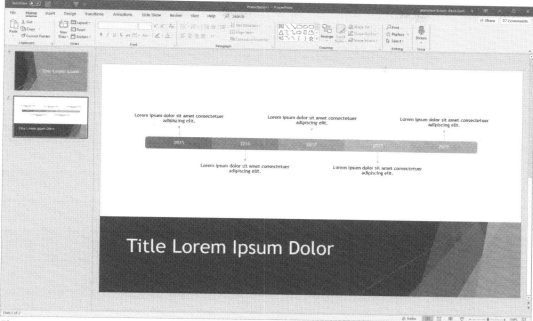

Figure 1.1

On the top of the program window, you will have your tabs and buttons which are on what is called the Ribbon (discussed in Chapter 2) and here is where all of your tools are located that you will use to add content to your presentation. If you use other Microsoft Office programs such as Word or Excel then you will be used to how the Ribbon works but will notice that the items contained on the Ribbon are different for the most part from other Office programs, but you will still find similar tools that you should recognize.

PowerPoint makes it easy to manipulate your text and images by simply clicking on them and doing things such as moving them, resizing them, moving them to a different slide or even deleting them just by clicking on them. It's much easier than it is with Word for example which takes a little more work to get similar results.

As you read through this book you should try out my examples for yourself because going through the process is the best way to learn how to use PowerPoint and you will find yourself getting very comfortable with the program in no time. You can also download sample presentations online and then edit them to practice some of the things you learned and even experiment by trying out any features you are interested in playing around with.

PowerPoint Alternatives

PowerPoint might be the most popular presentation software in use but it's not the only one out there by any means. So if you end up not liking PowerPoint, you can try some of the alternative presentation programs out there. Some are free and some you will have to pay for but regardless of which software you end up using, they will all most likely function in a similar fashion to PowerPoint.

I will now go over just a few of the PowerPoint alternatives but keep in mind that there are many more you can choose from. Some will be software you will install on your computer while others will be web based meaning you will use them in a web browser such as Google Chrome, Firefox, Edge, Safari, etc.

Google Slides

If you are familiar with Google Apps then you might have used their Google Docs (word processor) app or Google Sheets (spreadsheet) app on your computer, phone or tablet. Google also offers a free presentation app called *Google Slides* which is their version of PowerPoint. As you can see from figure 1.2 that it has the same look and feel as PowerPoint so it should be pretty easy to use if you are a PowerPoint user to begin with.

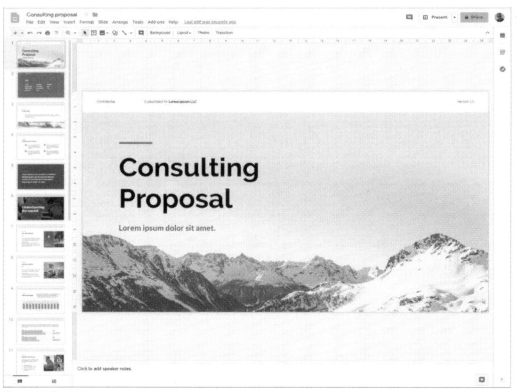

Figure 1.2

If you want to learn more about Google Apps and how they can make your life easier then you can check out my book called **Google Apps Made Easy**. These apps are free to use and all you need to do is have a free Google account to be able to access them.
https://www.amazon.com/dp/1798114992.

Prezi

Prezi is another online web based presentation app that is subscription based meaning you pay a monthly fee to use it rather than having to make a larger one time purchase of the software.

Prezi also has a similar look and feel to PowerPoint but works a little differently because it uses a canvas based approach rather than using slides. Prezi uses one canvas that your presentation moves around, and you then zoom in and out to view various frames.

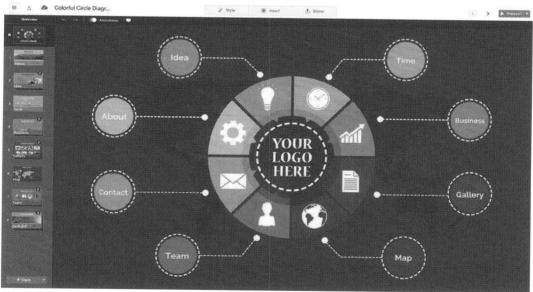

Figure 1.3

Here are the subscription costs for Prezi as of this writing.

- Standard Edition - $7/month
- Plus Edition - $19/month
- Premium Edition - $59/month

9

Visme

Visme is another web based presentation app that you can also use offline by downloading your presentation and then showing it via a web browser with no Internet connection required.

Figure 1.4

If you want to use the basic version then it is free but there are several other pay for versions that have additional features. Here is the breakdown of the plans and prices. You can go to their website for more details as to what is in each plan.

Individual Plans
- Basic - Free
- Standard - $14/month
- Complete - $25/month

Business Plans
- Single - $25/month
- Team - $75/month
- Enterprise – You need to contact them

Educational Plans
- Student - $30/semester
- Educator - $60/semester
- School – You need to contact them

Keynote (Mac)

Even though PowerPoint is made by Microsoft and so is Windows doesn't mean you can't use it on your Mac. But if you want to try some Apple based presentation software then you can try out Keynote. You can even save Keynote presentations so they can be used with PowerPoint in case you need to share them with a PowerPoint user.

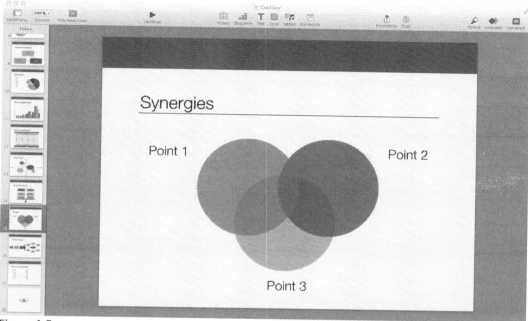

Figure 1.5

Keynote is free to use and might already be installed on your Apple device. If not then you can simply go to the App Store and download it and you will be ready to go!

Haiku Deck

Haiku Deck is another online presentation app that you can use in a web browser or on your smartphone or tablet. As you can see from figure 1.6, it looks a little different from the others in terms of how the interface is laid out. It doesn't use slides in order to avoid clutter and keep things simple but if you like the slide method or are used to using slides then it might not be for you.

Figure 1.6

Here is the pricing for Haiku Deck as of this writing.

- Pro - $9.95/month billed annually or $19.95/month billed monthly
- Premium - $29.95/month

PowerPoint Online

As you can see, there is a growing trend of using programs online and calling them apps that allows you to do your work from any Internet enabled device without having to install your presentation software on each one.

Well, this applies to PowerPoint as well and Microsoft actually has versions of most of their Office software online that you can use via your web browser or from an app that you can install on your smartphone or tablet.

If you have ever heard of Office 365, then this is the name Microsoft gives to their online suite of office productivity apps. These have the same look and feel as the Office programs you have installed on your computer (for the most part) but you can access them from anywhere you can sign into your online account with. It's also billed as a subscription rather than a one-time purchase.

But if you are the type who doesn't like to pay for stuff then there is also a free version you can use that doesn't have all the same bells and whistles as the Office 365 version but will work just fine for most people. The free Office Online site can be accessed from *https://products.office.com*. You will need a Microsoft account to access the apps though but that is free as well. If you have a Hotmail or Outlook.com email account then you can use that to log in with.

Figure 1.7 shows an example of what you will see when you log in. If you have used the online version of PowerPoint before then you will see any recent apps listed here. There are also many templates you can choose from to use when creating a new presentation.

Figure 1.7

Figure 1.8 shows the interface for the online version of PowerPoint and you can see that it's similar looking to the one you have on your computer but is just a little bit more simplified and it won't have all the same options.

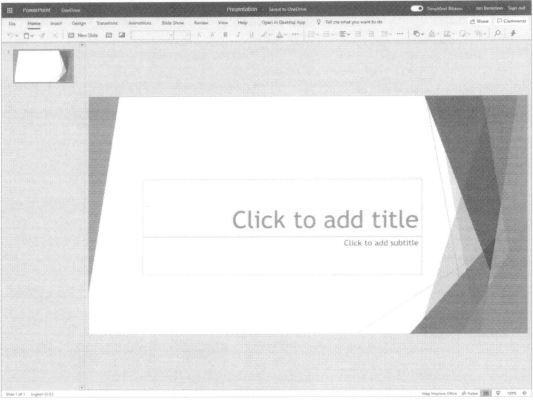

Figure 1.8

You can swap back and forth between the online version and the desktop version on your computer, but you will need to transfer the files somewhere such as your Microsoft OneDrive online storage account so the files are accessible online when you need to open them from the online version. You will automatically have a OneDrive account when you create your Microsoft account.

If you want to learn more about online storage apps such as OneDrive, Drobox, iCloud etc. then you can check out my book called *Cloud Storage Made Easy*. It covers the most popular cloud storage providers and teaches you how to use them.
https://www.amazon.com/dp/1730838359.

Chapter 2 – The PowerPoint Ribbon

Starting with Office 2007, Microsoft completely changed the user interface for its Office software, making many people very upset because they had to learn how to do everything all over again because they added what they called the Ribbon to all of their Office programs. If you have only worked with newer versions of Office, then you most likely don't know the difference and assume that the ribbon was always there.

Before I get into tabs and groups for PowerPoint in the next chapter, I want to discuss the Ribbon a bit. The Ribbon is the part of the program that has all of your icons, tabs, and groups for all of the different things you can do in PowerPoint. The Ribbon is shown in figure 2.1 and may look a little different depending on what version of PowerPoint you are using but should still function the same. Keep in mind that the ribbon for each program (such as Word vs. Excel) will have different options within their tabs and different tabs as well.

Figure 2.1

As you can see there are various tabs such as File, Home, Insert, Design and so on. In pre 2019 versions of PowerPoint, they looked more like actual tabs than they do now. Each tab has its own set of groups within it. For example, the Home tab contains the Clipboard, Slides, Font, Paragraph, Drawing and Editing groups. You can see the names of the groups at the bottom of the Ribbon.

Within many of the groups, there are other options that can be accessed by clicking on the arrow at the bottom right hand corner of the group. For example, clicking on this arrow in the Font group (figure 2.2) brings up the additional font options as shown in figure 2.3.

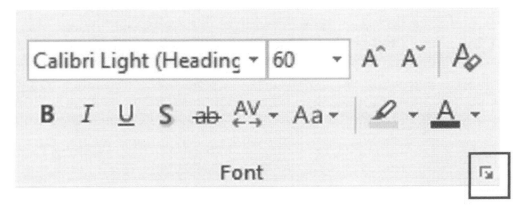

Figure 2.2

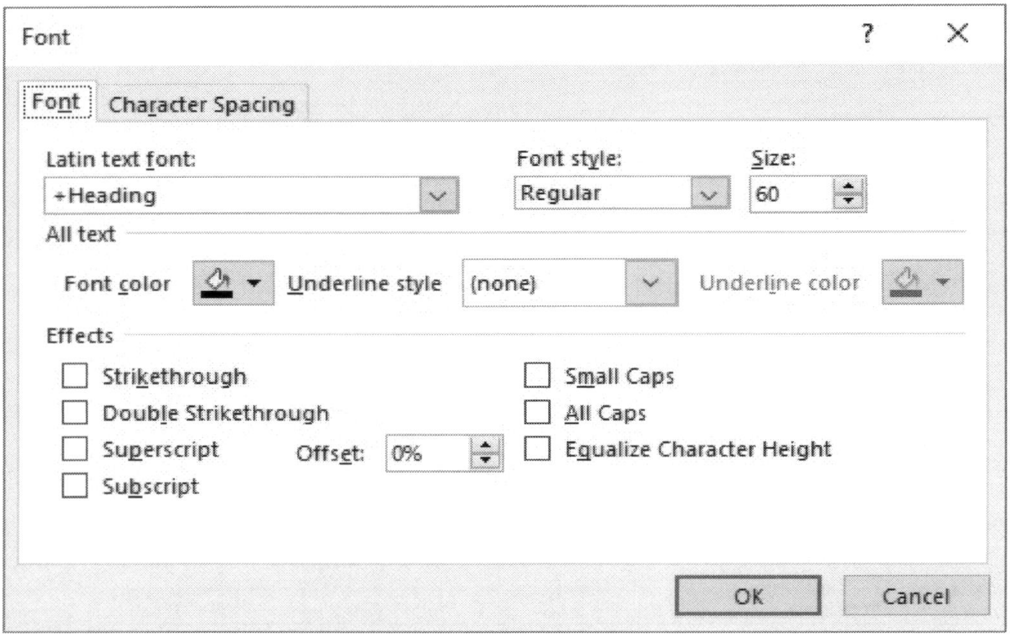

Figure 2.3

Customizing the Ribbon

The default ribbon settings will work fine for most people, but if you're the type that likes to customize things whenever possible, then you can add your own tabs and groups to the Ribbon. You can also remove some of the default tabs and groups if you desire.

To customize tabs and groups go to the File tab, click on Options and then click on the Customize Ribbon section. Take a look at figure 2.4 and you will see on the right side it shows your current tabs and then the current groups within those tabs. As you can see, the Home tab has groups named Clipboard, Slides, Font, Paragraph, Drawing, and Editing.

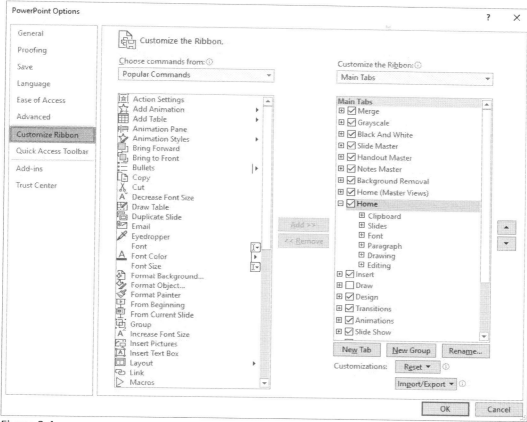

Figure 2.4

To add a new group to an existing tab, click on the tab's name to highlight it and then press the *New Group* button. Then name your group and insert commands from the left side list into your new group. As you can see in figure 2.5, I made a new group called Custom Group in the Home tab and added the Add Table and Email All Pages commands to that group. Then the results are shown in the ribbon (figure 2.6).

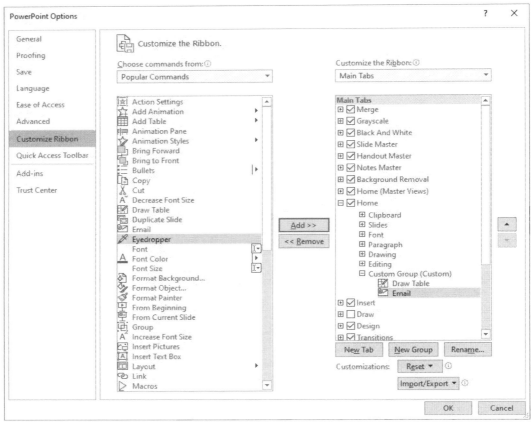

Figure 2.5

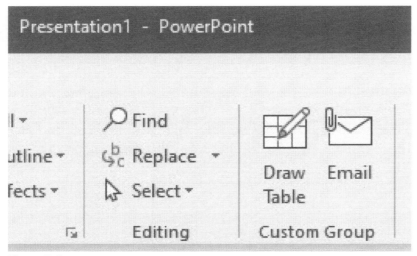

Figure 2.6

You can add and remove commands from a group by clicking on that group to highlight it, then finding the command you want from the left and clicking the *Add* button to add it to that group. You can also remove commands from the right by highlighting them and clicking the *Remove* button.

Adding a new tab is a similar process, and all you need to do is click on the tab you want to create a new tab next to, then click the *New Tab* button. In figure 2.7 you can see that I created a new tab called *Jim's* next to the Home tab. Then I created a group within this tab called *Jim's Group* and added the Bring to Front and Group commands to that group. Figure 2.8 shows the results of this new tab creation in the Ribbon.

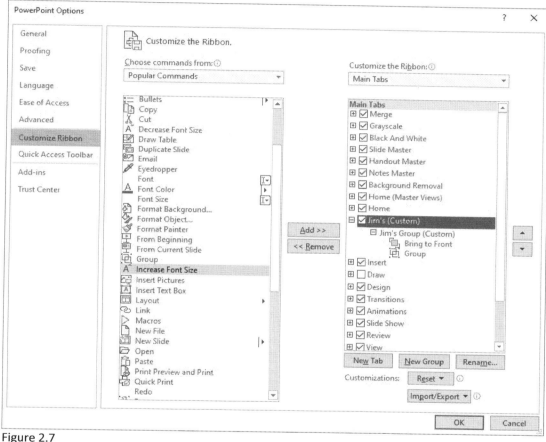

Figure 2.7

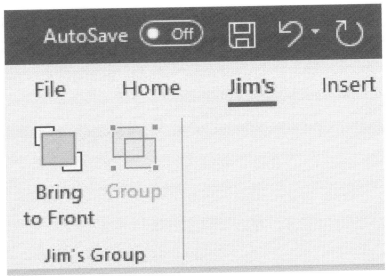

Figure 2.8

Quick Launch Bar

One very useful area of the Ribbon that you will find yourself using all the time is called the Quick Launch Bar. Think of the Quick Launch Bar as the place where you will go to perform the actions that you use the most, such as save, open, and print. If you take a look at figure 2.9, you will see a bunch of icons at the top above the tabs next to where it says AutoSave. These are your Quick Launch icons and, as you can see, it makes it easy to group all of the icons you use the most in one place.

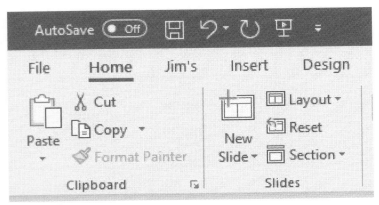

Figure 2.9

The icons do not have names, but since they are the ones you will use all the time, you will get to know exactly what each one does. Plus, if you hover the mouse pointer over the icon, it will tell you what it is used for. If you click the little down arrow to the right of the icons it will bring up a list of all the Quick Launch commands that you have available on your Quick Launch Bar (figure 2.10). Then you can check the ones you want displayed on the Quick Launch Bar or uncheck ones that you don't want to show.

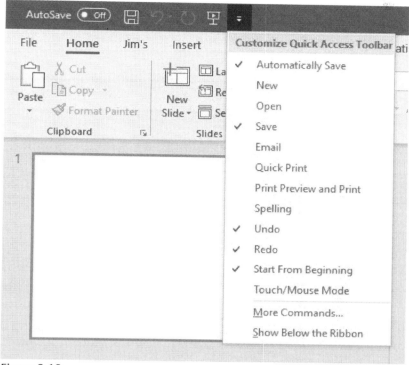

Figure 2.10

If you click on Show Below the Ribbon it will put your Quick Launch icons underneath the ribbon (as shown in figure 2.11).

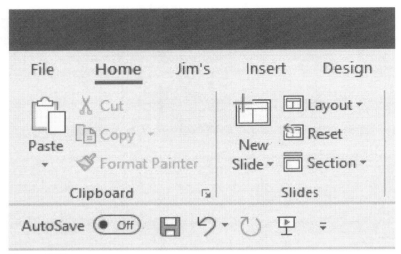

Figure 2.11

Customizing the Quick Launch Bar

Just like with tabs and groups, it's possible to customize the Quick Launch Bar to your liking. When clicking on the down arrow next to the icons (as shown in figure 2.10) there is a choice called *More Commands*. This will take you to the Quick Access Toolbar customization setting, which you can also get to from the File tab and then Options (figure 2.12).

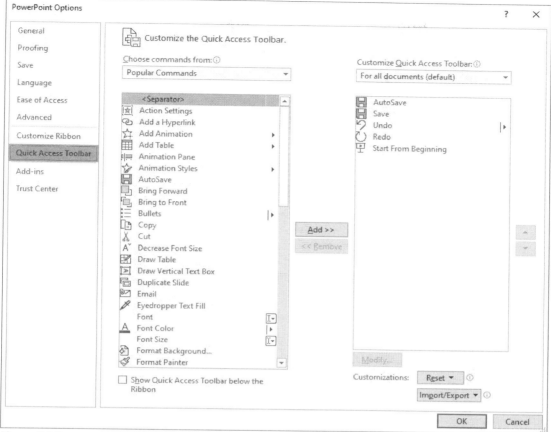

Figure 2.12

From here you can add commands from the right or remove commands from the left. You can also choose if the Quick Launch icons apply to the current document you are working on or all documents that you create or open.

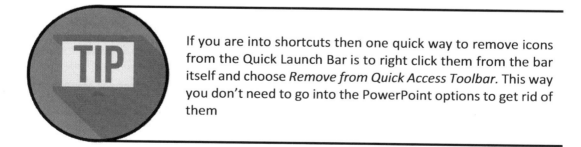

If you are into shortcuts then one quick way to remove icons from the Quick Launch Bar is to right click them from the bar itself and choose *Remove from Quick Access Toolbar.* This way you don't need to go into the PowerPoint options to get rid of them

If you have made changes to the Ribbon or Quick Launch Bar and want to revert things back to the Office default, simply go to the options for either one and then click the button on the bottom of the window that says *Reset* (as you can see in figure 2.12).

One nice feature that Office programs have is that you can import and export your custom settings to be used on another computer that has Office installed. That way you don't need to configure the other computer from scratch if you have made a lot of changes that you like to use.

Hiding the Ribbon

If for some reason, you would like some more real estate on your screen and think the Ribbon is in the way, then it's possible to collapse the Ribbon and only have it show when you need it.

To do so you can press *Ctrl-F1* on your keyboard when you want to hide the Ribbon, or you can click the small up arrow at the very bottom right of the ribbon to collapse it. Then press Ctrl-F1 to bring it back, or right click any tab and clear the checkmark next to *Collapse the Ribbon*. You can also double click any tab to have the ribbon brought back on the screen.

There are also some additional configurations you can set for what shows on the ribbon. If you click on the icon that looks like a box with an arrow in it (figure 2.13) you will be able to set some additional options. You can have Office auto hide the ribbon, show tabs only, or show the tabs with their commands (which is the default).

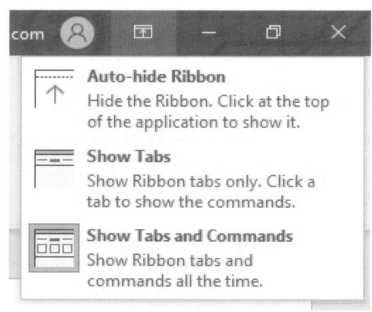

Figure 2.13

Chapter 3 – Tabs and Groups

Like I mentioned earlier, PowerPoint has its own unique tabs compared to the other Office programs but there are also some different groups within the tabs that are common to the other Office programs. In this chapter, I will be going over the tabs within PowerPoint and also the groups contained in these tabs.

File Tab

The File tab is used for things you will do before and after working on your presentation. As you can see in figure 3.1, you have various options to choose from such as opening, saving, and printing your presentations. Most of these options are obvious, but I want to go over a few that might not be.

Figure 3.1

Info

This section will give you specific information about the presentation you are working on such as its size, the number of slides, last modified date, created date, the author, and so on.

- **Protect Presentation** – This is where you can do things such as protect your presentation with a password and restrict editing so nobody can make unauthorized changes.

- **Inspect Presentation** – Here you can have PowerPoint check your presentation to make sure it's compatible with older versions of PowerPoint, or to make sure people with disabilities won't find it hard to read.

- **Manage Presentation** – If you are using a document server, you will have check in and check out options here. And, if you have any unsaved presentation that can be recovered, you can look at them here as well.

Save As

PowerPoint allows you to save presentations in other formats besides the default PowerPoint format. You might have noticed that your PowerPoint presentations end in .pptx, which is the default file extension for PowerPoint. If you look at figure 3.2, you can see there are many other formats to choose from, such as a .ppt version to be compatible with older versions of PowerPoint, PDF file, image file, video file and so on. I will be going over these save options in more detail in Chapter 7.

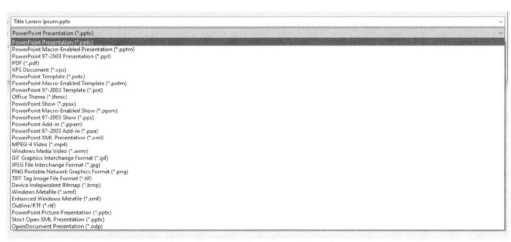

Figure 3.2

Share

If you are the type that's into saving your files "in the cloud" then you have that option in the Share section. The Share options will most likely be different depending on what version of PowerPoint you are using. Microsoft likes to push its users to use its online storage service called *OneDrive* which is similar to other online storage services like Dropbox and iCloud. It's free to use so you don't need to worry about spending money to take advantage of it. When you click on Share you might be prompted to sign into your OneDrive account to upload your presentation to your online drive. You can also share it via an email message as well. I will get into more details on sharing in Chapter 7.

Export

This section is similar to the Save As section where you can save your presentation in a different format, except here you are exporting it rather than saving it. Once again, I will be covering this in more detail in Chapter 7.

Home Tab

Like all the other Office programs, the Home tab is the default tab that is displayed when you open the program. The Home tab contains many of the more commonly used settings, and that's why Microsoft has made it the default tab when you open any of their software. It has many of the same groups as the other Office programs, but there are some that are specific to PowerPoint and they should be pretty obvious as we go along. For example, the Slides group sounds like the type of group that would be specific to PowerPoint since we use slides within the program.

Figure 3.3

Now I will go over each group within the Home tab.

Clipboard

The clipboard is used to hold information such as copied text and images to keep them in memory until you are ready to paste them into your presentation or somewhere else. The clipboard will paste the last copied item unless you expand the Clipboard group by clicking on the little arrow to show other items you have copied. From this section, you can paste in different formats, depending on what you are pasting.

Slides

The Slides group is where you can add new slides and keep things organized. There are four main tools you can use in this group:

- **New Slide** – If you want to add another slide into your presentation, simply click the New Slide button to add a new blank slide, or you can click the down arrow to choose from preconfigured slide templates. You can also choose to duplicate the slide you have selected or reuse a slide from a different PowerPoint file.

- **Layout** – Here you can change the layout of an existing slide to one of the preconfigured layouts included with PowerPoint.

- **Reset** – This setting will reset the position, size, and formatting of the slide placeholders to their default setting. So, if you make a bunch of changes and want to start over, then you can use the Reset feature.

- **Section** – When you have a lot of slides sometimes it's a good idea to break them up into sections to keep them more organized. In figure 3.4, you can see how the slides are broken up into sections called Day 1 and Day 2.

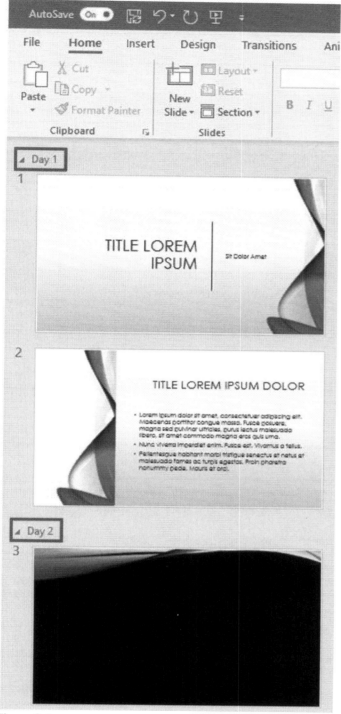

Figure 3.4

Font

Fonts, also known as typestyles, are used to change how the characters look on the screen and when printed. Windows comes with its own default fonts installed and many programs will install additional fonts when you install the actual program, so not every computer will have the same fonts. From the Font section, you can do things such as change the font type, color, and size.

Paragraph

Here you can adjust settings to change the text to align to the left or right, be centered, or be justified on both sides. You can also set text indents, line and paragraph spacing, and create borders from this section.

Drawing

Once you start using PowerPoint you will find yourself using the Drawing group quite a bit. When people make presentations, they like to include lots of arrows, lines, boxes, and so on to get their point across. Once you draw your shape, you can click on it to highlight it (as shown in figure 3.5). Then you can resize it and rotate it to suit your needs.

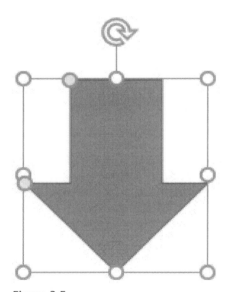

Figure 3.5

If you click on the arrow at the bottom right of the Drawing group it will bring up the Format Shape settings (figure 3.6), where you can change things such as fill color, line color and size, effects, and so on. There are also some buttons for these features in the Drawing group itself.

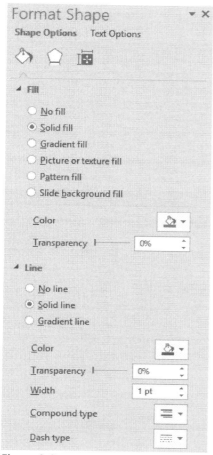

Figure 3.6

If you are looking for a quick way to add some color to your drawing, PowerPoint also has some built-in styles that you can apply to your drawing from the *Quick Styles* button which is located within this group.

Editing

If you have a lot of text and want to find a word or phrase to maybe change it or remind yourself if you even typed it at all, you can use the *Find* feature from the Editing group. Simply click on *Find*, type in the information you are searching for, and it will show you all the results in the document. Then you can click on a particular result and it will take you right to it within the document. The *Replace* feature is great to use if you want to replace a certain word with another throughout the whole document. For example, let's say you spelled Jon as John and want to replace all the instances of John with Jon. You can do that with the Replace tool.

Insert Tab

When using PowerPoint you will be inserting many items such as pictures, text, drawings, etc. into your presentation so you will be using the Insert tab quite a bit. Now I will go over each of the groups within the Insert tab.

Figure 3.7

New Slide

It should be pretty obvious that this is used to insert a new slide into your presentation. It will add the slide below the currently highlighted slide. As you can see, you have several options when inserting a new slide. You can even duplicate existing slides if you want to save yourself some work rather than recreating them on a new blank slide.

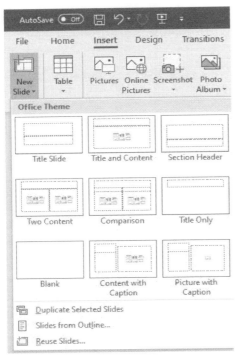

Figure 3.8

Tables

Tables come in handy if you want to create a spreadsheet style table to store information to use in an easy to read format. You can create tables of almost any size and then customize them after they are created. You can either draw your own table or have one created by entering in the specifications you need (figure 3.9).

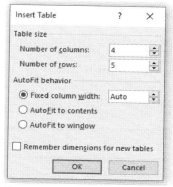

Title 1	Title 2	Title 3	Title 4
Data	Data	Data	Data
Data	Data	Data	Data
Data	Data	Data	Data
Data	Data	Data	Data
Data	Data	Data	Data

Figure 3.9

Images

When you want to insert a picture into your presentation, you will go to the Images group to do so. From here you have several options to choose from as to where you are getting your images from.

- **Pictures** – With this option you can simply select images from your computer by browsing to the folder on your hard drive where you have them stored.

- **Online Pictures** – Here you can have PowerPoint search the Internet for pictures based on a search term and then you can insert them into your slide.

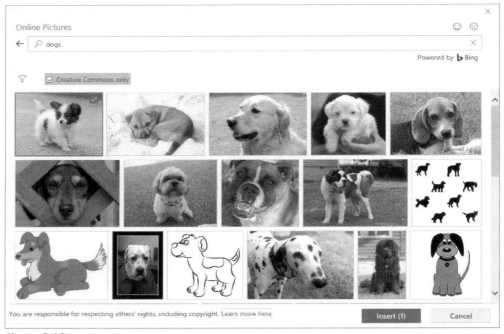

Figure 3.10

- **Screenshot** – This option will let you choose from any of the last several screenshots or images that you might have captured on your clipboard while working on your computer. You can also use the *Screen Clipping* tool to capture a screenshot on the spot.

- **Photo Album** – Here you can choose photos from your computer and have PowerPoint create a photo album for you by placing each one on a separate slide. All you need to do is browse to the location where you have the pictures stored and choose the ones you want in the album and PowerPoint will do the rest. Figure 3.11 shows the results after I chose four images for my photo album. PowerPoint even creates a title slide for you, and you can change how it looks by using one of the built in styles after you create the album.

Figure 3.11

Illustrations

Besides photos, it's a very common practice to insert things like shapes and charts into your documents, and the Illustration group is one that you will most likely be using a lot.

- **Shapes** - Shapes are another item that is commonly inserted into documents. Many people like to draw arrows, lines, boxes, and other shapes to highlight important information in their documents.

- **Icons** – Icons are kind of like clipart that you can insert into your slides. You can choose from one of the many built in categories or do a search for a specific type of icon.

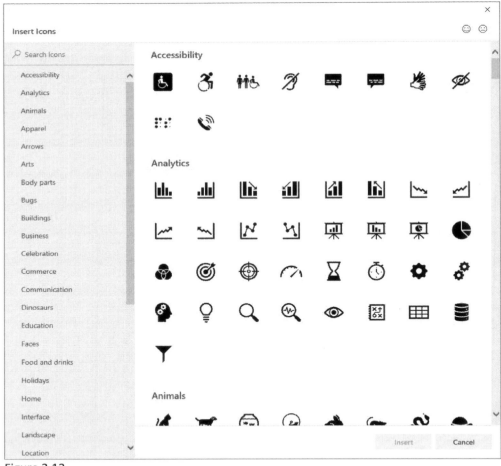

Figure 3.12

- **3D Models** – 3d Models consist of models of various things such as people, animals, buildings that you can manipulate by moving them around in all directions to see every side of the model. Some of them are even animated. You can import them manually if you have your own models or search for one online.

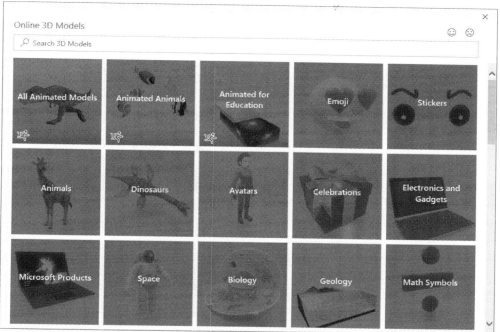

Figure 3.13

Once you insert your model you can then do things like resize and rotate it to better fit your presentation.

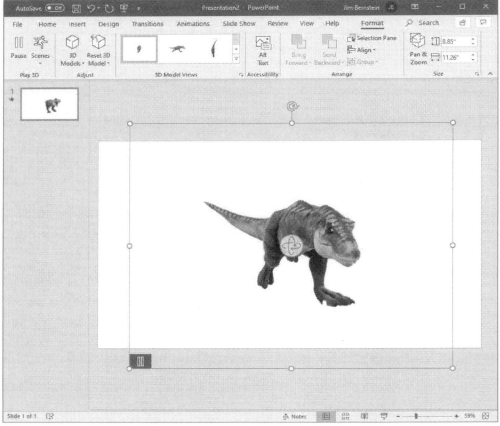

Figure 3.14

- **SmartArt** - SmartArt is a way to insert graphics based on certain categories such as hierarchy and pyramids.

- **Charts** - Charts can be used to insert Excel-like information without having to link your document to an Excel file. After you choose your chart type and insert it, you can then edit the values and data for your chart.

Add-ins
This group is not used too often unless you have installed some add-ins to your software. Add-ins will add additional features such as file conversion tools, additional clipart, language translators, training, and more. If you click on the *Get Add-ins* you will be taken to the add-ins store where you can install any add-ins you want to try. Keep in mind that many are free, but there are some that will cost you money to use.

Links
If you have ever used a web browser to go online then you should be familiar with the concept of links. Links consist of text or images that you can click on to take you

to another page on a website, another website altogether or even another part of your PowerPoint presentation. PowerPoint has three types of links that you can use within your presentation.

- **Zoom** – There are three types of Zoom features in the Links section and each one works a little differently.

  - *Summary Zoom* – This creates a summary slide that you can use to zoom in and out of different slide groupings. For example, let's say I have a presentation with three chapters, I can use the Summary Zoom to select the slides with the chapter titles on them and then click the *Insert* button.

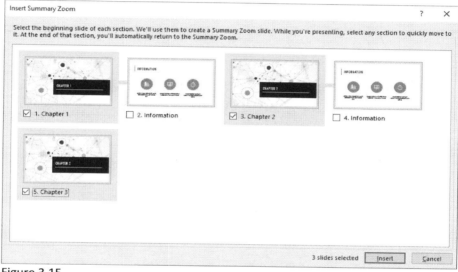

Figure 3.15

Then it would make a new slide at the top of my slide deck with each one of those slides on it and I would be able to click on any one of them to be taken to that chapter (figure 3.16).

CHAPTERS

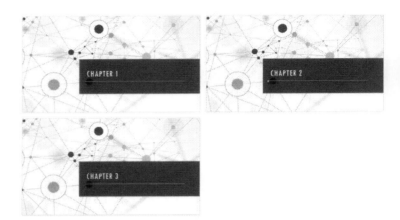

Figure 3.16

- o *Section Zoom* – These are used to link to a section you already have in your presentation. They are also used to emphasize certain areas of your presentation and make it easy to go right to the section you want to discuss. If you don't have any sections in your presentation you will not be able to use this feature. Sections were discussed earlier in this chapter.

- o *Slide Zoom* – This can be used to take you to a particular slide or section and have the presentation continue from there. For example, you might want to have the last slide of your presentation contain some links to other slides or sections so you can then review them just by clicking on them.

  Figure 3.17 shows my final slide named Important Concepts and I will use the Slide Zoom feature to add slides 1, 6 and 8 to the slide itself.

Important Concepts

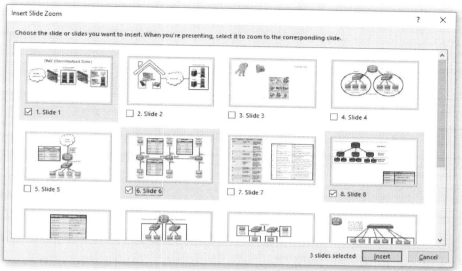

Figure 3.17

Important Concepts

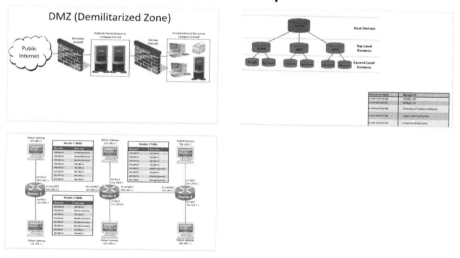

Figure 3.18

Now my slide has thumbnail images for each of the three slides I chose to add to it, and I can then click on any one of them during my presentation and be taken to that slide.

 When you are using the Zoom feature you can go to the Zoom tools under the Format tab that appears when you click on one of your zoom slides and then check the box that says *Return to zoom*. Doing this will make it so when you are done clicking through that section PowerPoint will return to the thumbnail view of the zoom slides.

- **Link** – If you want to insert a simple text link to a web page, existing file or email address you can do so from the Link option. Just highlight the text in your presentation you want to be the link and then click on *Link>Insert Link* and choose the type of link you wish to create. If you want to link to a website then type in its address in the *Address* box. The *Text to display* area will be taken from the text you highlighted in PowerPoint but can be changed if you desire.

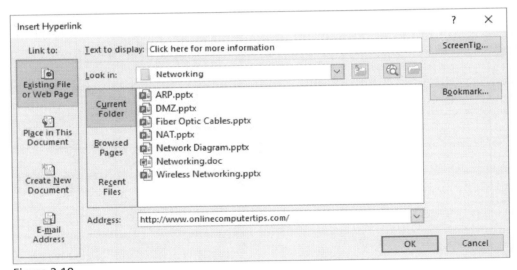

Figure 3.19

Choosing *Place in This Document* will allow you to have the link take you to a particular slide when clicked on.

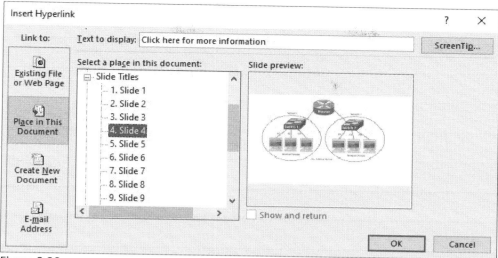

Figure 3.20

The E-mail Address section allows you to enter an email address and subject that will pop up when the link is clicked on so that person can send an email right to the address you added to the link.

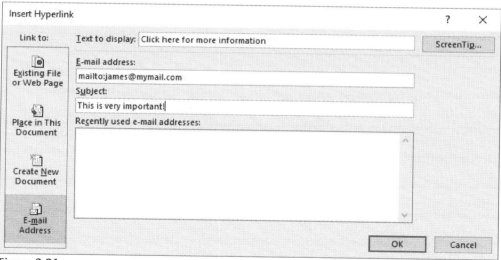

Figure 3.21

- **Action** – Actions are used to take a particular action when an object is clicked on or when you hover the mouse over the object (picture or text, etc.). To use this feature simply click on the object in your presentation that you want to have the action taken on and then click on the *Action* button.

You will then be prompted to choose what type of action to take on that object. Some of the things you can do include having PowerPoint go to a particular slide, run a specific program, play a sound and so on.

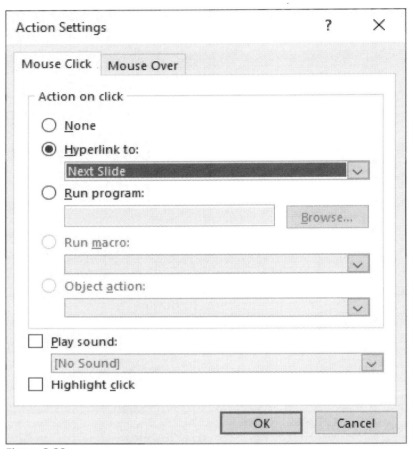

Figure 3.22

Comments
Comments are used to add comments to your slide, which will appear off to the right in a special margin. They are usually used when reviewing a document and making a note of such things as errors or changes.

Text
The Text group has a variety of text related items you can add to your presentation. There are various text related activities you can perform from this group.

- **Text Box** – This choice lets you add text within a box that you can move around the screen and place on top of images. You can then format the text in the box any way you like and also format the text box itself to remove the box around the text.

- **Header & Footer** – Headers and footers are used to label slides with various types of information and work the same way they do in other Office programs such as Word.

- **Word Art** – WordArt has been around for some time, but it is still a cool way to add some flash to your slides. All you need to do is click on a WordArt style you like and start typing. Then you can drag your new text box around the screen and place it wherever you want on your slide, as shown below.

- **Date & Time** – If you would like the current date and time placed on your slides you can add it from here.

- **Slide Number** – If you want page numbers on your slides you can add them from here.

- **Object** – Another feature of the Text group includes the ability to embed (insert) other types of documents such as Word files or PDFs within your primary document so they can be opened right off the page itself.

Symbols
These are used when you need to add a specific kind of character to your document such as ©™ π. Equations can be inserted as well if you are the smart type that has a use for that!

Media
Photos, video and audio are a big part of PowerPoint presentations and the Media section is where you need to go if you want to add any videos, music, voice recordings and so on to your masterpiece.

- **Video** – Here you have the option to insert a video from a file on your computer or you can also insert one from an online source such as YouTube. To do this you will need to know the URL (address) of the video and enter into the box as shown in figure 3.23.

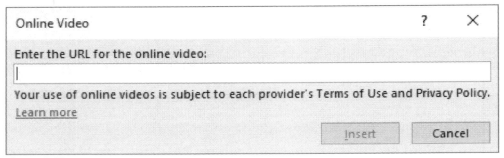

Figure 3.23

- **Audio** – The Audio feature allows you to insert an audio file such as an MP3 into your presentation, or you can record some audio on the spot assuming you have a microphone attached to your computer.

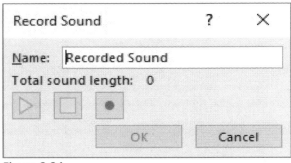

Figure 3.24

- **Screen Recording** – This feature is really cool because you can have PowerPoint take a video recording of what you are doing on your screen and then insert it into your presentation as a video that you can play back. So, if you need to demonstrate something for training purposes, it's a great way to do so.

Design Tab

There aren't really too many things to do here except change the way your overall slides look when it comes to their design. There are a bunch of built-in themes you can choose from, and as you click on each one it will change your whole presentation and give you a preview of what it will look like (figure 3.25).

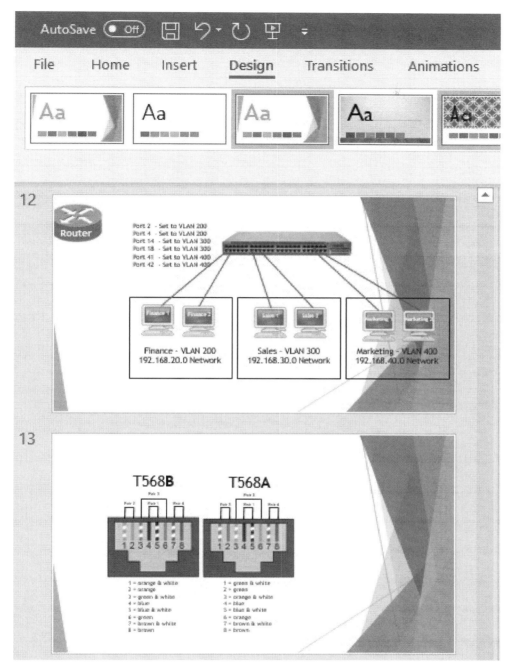

Figure 3.25

By default, PowerPoint uses a widescreen (16:9) size for its slides, but if you want something a little squarer you can choose the standard (4:3) or create your own custom size from the *Customize* group.

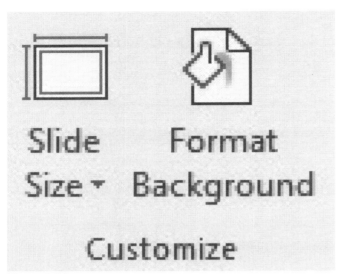

Figure 3.26

Clicking the *Format Background* button in the Customize group will bring up settings to change your background in regards to color, transparency, brightness, gradients, and so on.

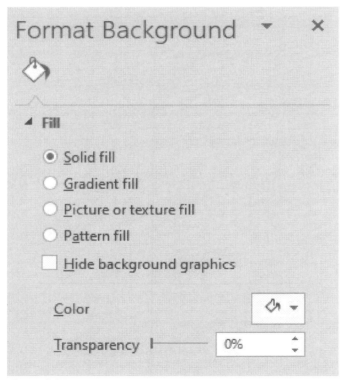

Figure 3.27

Transitions Tab

Transitions are used to create effects that take place in between your slides. There are many built-in transitions you can apply and once you choose one of these transitions you can customize it even further.

Figure 3.28

To use transitions, select the slide you want the transition to take place on. Then choose a transition you like and click on the *Preview* button on the left to see how it will look when applied. Then, under *Effect Options*, choose whether you want the transition to happen smoothly, or if you want it to fade to black between the slides. I will be covering transitions in more detail in Chapter 6.

Timing

The Timing group is where you can go to set how fast and with what action your slides will transition from one to the other. The *Duration* setting is set at one second by default, but if you want to be more dramatic and extend that time period, then enter however many seconds you like. There is also an option to have a sound play in between each slide, such as a drumroll. Keep in mind that using sounds might get annoying after a while unless you do it for just a couple of slides to make a point.

By default, PowerPoint won't advance to the next slide during a slide show unless you click the mouse, but if you want your slide show to run automatically, then you can check the box labeled *After* and enter the time interval between slides.

Once you get things looking the way you want them, you can click on the *Apply To All* button to have your settings be applied to your entire presentation.

Animations Tab

Animations are a big part of PowerPoint slide shows, and you will find yourself on the Animations tab on a regular basis. Animations are when you have one aspect of your slide show change into another, such as some text sliding off the screen and an image appearing in its place.

As you can see from figure 3.29, the Animations tab looks similar to the Transition tab, and it functions the same way (to some degree) and there are several groups under this tab that I will quickly go over since I will be covering animations in more detail in Chapter 6.

Figure 3.29

Animation
Under the Animation group there are many built-in animations that you can apply to your slides, and there is also the *Preview* button like we saw on the Transitions tab. The *Effect Options* button will let you fine tune how the animation you chose will play out such as the direction that the animation moves etc. The options will be different based on your choice of animation.

Advanced Animation
If you click on the *Animation Pane* button it will open up an area on the side of your slide where you will have a listing of all the animations you have applied to that slide. From here you can fine tune the way each one of your animations work such as having them be triggered with a mouse click or after a certain amount of time.

The *Trigger* button can be used to tell PowerPoint at what point to start the animation such as when you click on a certain picture or text box. The *Animation Painter* can be used to copy animations from one object to another saving you time when you want to apply duplicate animations to other objects in your presentation.

Timing
The settings in the Timing group include options to control when the animation begins, the duration of the animation, and also its delay. You can also change the order of your animations within the *Reorder Animation* section by clicking on the animation from the Animation Pane and then choosing either *Move Earlier* or *Move Later*.

Slide Show Tab
The whole point of making a PowerPoint presentation is so you can show it to other people in the form of a slide show, so it makes sense to have a tab dedicated to how your slide show will appear when you play it.

Figure 3.30

Start Slide Show
This group will allow you to decide how the slide show is presented and when it starts. The *From Begging* button will start the slide show from the first slide while the *From Current Slide* button will start it from whatever slide you are on while in editing mode. If you have access to the Office Presentation Service (which is free, by the way), then you can upload your slide show so it can be viewed online via a web browser by other people who might not be in your office. Finally, the *Custom Slide Show* option will let you choose which slides you want to appear in your slide show just in case there are some you want to omit.

Set Up
This group is where you adjust your settings for showing how the slide show will start, and how it will play once you get it going. There are several settings you can adjust here:

- **Set Up Slide Show** – When you click on this button you will be presented with the options shown in figure 3.31, and from here you can choose the type of show, the show options, what slides will be shown, how the slides will be advanced, and if the show will be presented on multiple monitors.

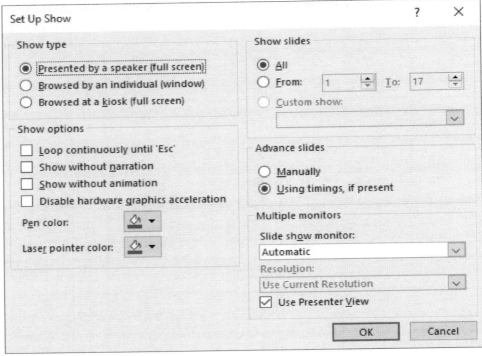

Figure 3.31

- **Hide Slide** – If there's a particular slide you don't want to appear when you run your slide show then select that slide and click on the Hide Slide button to prevent it from showing.

- **Rehearse Timings** – If you plan on running your slide show automatically, then you will want to have an idea of how much time you'll need to spend on each slide. With the Rehearse Timings option, you can run through your slides and PowerPoint will track how much time you spend between each one Then you can save the timing, and have it applied to your automatic slide show.

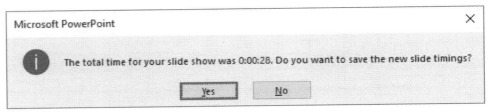

Figure 3.32

- **Record Slide Show** – With this option, you can have PowerPoint record your slide show along with any voice narrations and webcam footage so you can show it later. While recording the slide show you will have a Recording box in the upper left hand corner where you can pause the recording or advance to the next slide or animation if needed. You can also click with the mouse to advance the slides.

Figure 3.33

While recording you can right click anywhere on the slide, choose *Pointer Options,* and select from tools such as a laser pointer, pen, or highlighter. Then you can play your slide show back with your narrations and highlights to see how it looks.

- **Play Narrations** – If you have recorded any narrations for your presentation you can have them enabled or disabled by checking or unchecking this box.

- **Use Timings** – Here you can control whether or not any custom animation timings you have created are used or not when playing your slide show.

- **Show Media Controls** – When you insert media into your slides such as videos or audio there will be buttons for doing things such as playing and pausing the media during the slide show and you can use this checkbox to have them shown or hidden.

Monitors

The final group in the Slide Show tab is the *Monitors* group, and here is where you can tell PowerPoint how you want the slide show to be presented if you have more than one monitor. The options are *Automatic* or *Primary Monitor,* which will allow you to select which one of your monitors the slide show plays on. *Use Presenter View* allows you to have the slide show on one monitor while showing things like notes and a preview of the next slide (etc.) on the other monitor.

Review Tab

Sometimes people have the need to have their presentations proofed or reviewed so they send them out for someone else to look over. Or, there may be a time when you need to send your presentation to your supervisor for approval and changes before showing it to a client. This is where the Review tab comes into play. It lets the reviewer check the presentation and make markups to show suggested changes that can be sent back to the creator of the presentation. There are various groups within the Review tab that I will now go over.

Figure 3.34

Proofing

This group should be pretty obvious as to what it does. You have your spelling and grammar checker as well as use a thesaurus if needed.

Accessibility

You can use the Accessibility Checker to have PowerPoint check your presentation for any errors that might make it difficult for people to follow along with. Figure 3.36 shows the results of the Accessibility Checker with some of the results expanded after I ran it against one of my presentations.

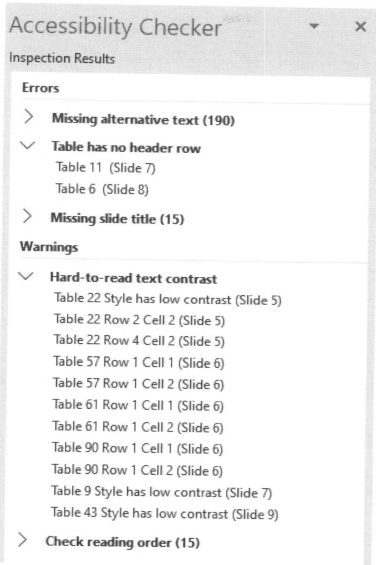

Figure 3.35

Insights

The Insights feature is kind of interesting because you can highlight a word or phrase, click the *Smart Lookup* button, and PowerPoint will go out on the Internet and find you some information about whatever you have highlighted. For example, I typed in *Microsoft PowerPoint*, highlighted the text, and clicked the Smart Lookup button and figure 3.36 shows the results.

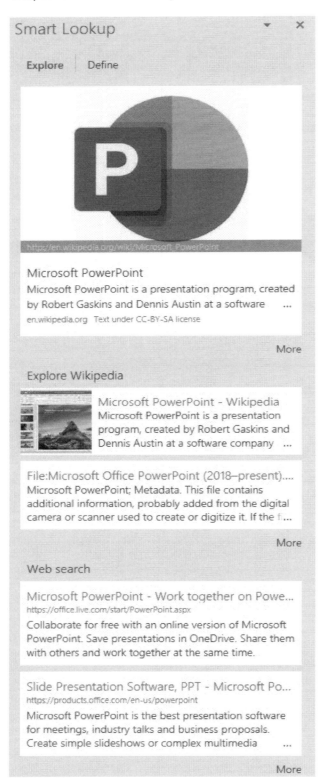

Figure 3.36

Language

The Language group has a cool feature called the *Translator* which allows you to highlight text in your presentation and then have it translated to a language of your choice. You can also manually type in text in the box once you have the Translator open.

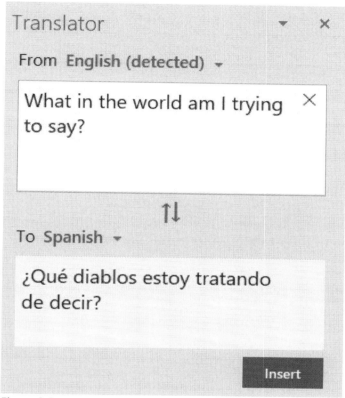

Figure 3.37

The Language part of the Language group will let you change the proofing language if you have a presentation in a different language for example. It will also take you to the PowerPoint language options in case you want to make any adjustments there.

Comments

If you are reviewing a presentation for someone, you can make comments on certain text that you want the person who you are going to send the document to read. Click on *New Comment* to add a new comment, and PowerPoint will add a comment section to the right of the page. The *Delete* button will allow you to delete a comment or all of your comments, and the *Previous* and *Next* buttons will scroll through your comments in case you want to review them yourself. If you want to see the comments that the reviewer has made to your presentation then you can click on the *Show Comments* button and as you scroll through the slides.

Compare

After the reviewer makes their changes and you accept or reject their changes, you most likely will have two different versions of the same presentation. The *Compare* section will allow you to either compare both versions to see the differences or combine both versions into one presentation.

Ink

If you have a digital pen or other input device installed on your computer then you can use the Ink feature to actually draw on your slides. Then if you want to hide any ink that you have drawn, you can do so from here.

View Tab

Not everyone likes to view their work the same way and fortunately PowerPoint makes it easy to change how the program looks while doing your work. This way you can be as efficient as possible and be able to get your presentation created without too much difficulty.

Figure 3.38

Presentation Views

Just like with the other Office programs, PowerPoint has its own set of views that you can choose from to change how your presentation looks on the screen. Most of the time you will be using *Normal View,* which shows the slide previews on the left of the screen and the slide you are working on in the center. In *Outline View,* you can do things like add notes to your slides and create outlines that you can edit from this view by right clicking on the outline and choosing one of the available options (figure 3.39).

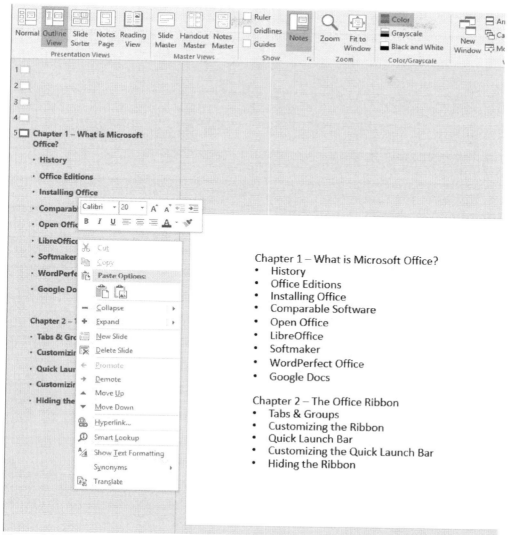

Figure 3.39

After you create your slides, you might need to rearrange them, and the best way to do that is to use the *Slide Sorter* view. Then you can drag and drop the slides in the order you want them to appear (figure 3.40).

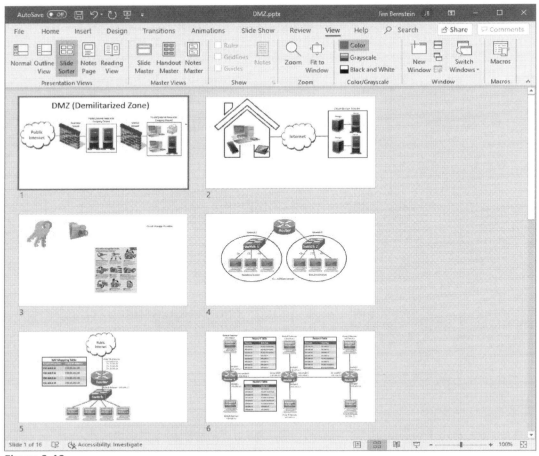

Figure 3.40

After you make some notes on your slides you can see how they will look when printed out with the presentation by using the *Notes Page* view.

Finally, you can use the *Reading View* to see how your slide show will play out in the current window without having to switch to the full screen slide show mode.

Master Views
When creating PowerPoint files, it's important to retain consistency among your slides when it comes to fonts, colors, logos, and so on to keep things looking professional. The *Slide Master* controls how all these visual features look throughout the entire presentation. Once you are in the Slide Master view, you will have the master slide listed on top with sub slides showing below. When you make a change to the Slide Master, it will take effect on all of the other slides below it. It won't change the content of the slides, but only their appearance.

When you click on *Close Master View*, these changes will be applied to your slides. I will be covering Slide Masters in more detail in Chapter 5.

If you plan on printing out your slide show to hand out to viewers then you can click the *Handout Master* button to see how it will look when printed. You can also make changes here, as well as change the page setup options. The *Notes Master* does a similar thing but will let you adjust how things will look when printed out with any notes you might have with your slides. The *Notes* button in the Show group will toggle the note box on or off for the slide.

Show
PowerPoint has some features that you can use to help you fine tune the placement of your text, photos and other objects to help give your presentation a consistent look and feel.

Figure 3.41 shows a slide with all of the features of the Show group enabled. As you can see there is a ruler on the left hand side of the slide as well as at the top. You can also see that there are gridlines going vertically and horizontally over the entire slide making boxes that you can use to help line up your objects. The guidelines are going through the middle of the slide and there is one that is horizontal and one that is vertical. You can move these guidelines to wherever you need them to be. Finally, the Notes option is enabled and the note I have for this slide is shown underneath the slide at the bottom.

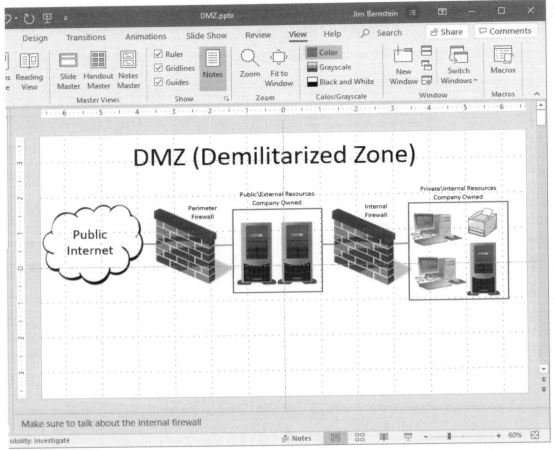

Figure 3.41

Zoom
This section should be pretty obvious as to what it does. You can click on the *Zoom* magnifying glass icon to zoom into a slide or you can click the *Fit to Window* button to have the entire slide fit on the screen, so you don't have to do any scrolling.

Color/Grayscale
If for some reason you don't want your presentation to be in color, you can click on *Grayscale* or *Black and White* to have the color removed from your slides. When you do this the Ribbon options will change as shown in figure 3.42 and you will have a bunch of options to fine tune the shades of grey for you slides if you will.

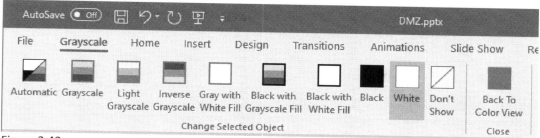

Figure 3.42

Some of the options won't change the way your slides look depending on how they were set up to begin with. Figure 3.43 shows what my slide looks like after clicking on Black in the Grayscale tab.

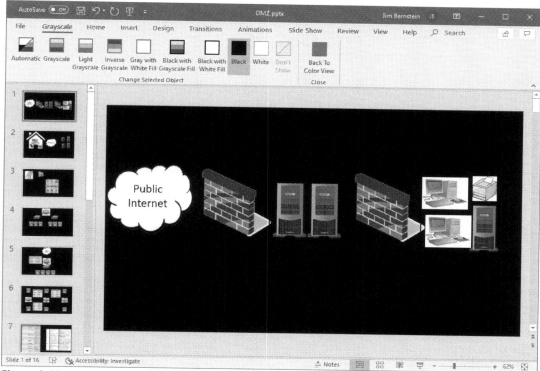

Figure 3.43

If you want your colors back simply click on the *Back to Color View* button.

Changing the view to greyscale or black and white will not affect how your presentation prints. If you want to print your slides in black and white you will need to change the settings during the printing process.

Window

The Window group allows you to change the views when you have more than one presentation open. You have several views to choose from:

- **New Window** – This will open the existing presentation in a new window. When you make changes to the presentation in one window, the other window will update the changes.

- **Arrange All** – This view will arrange all the presentations on your screen so you can see all of them. If you have too many presentations open at one time, this view doesn't do a lot of good.

- **Cascade** – This view will show all of your open presentations overlapping each other on the screen.

- **Switch Windows** – If you have multiple presentations open, you can click on this button to switch back and forth between them.

- **Move Split** – Splitters are the areas between two panes in your presentation. For example, there is a splitter between the slide deck on the left side of the screen and the slide you are working on. If you want to increase or decrease the size of one of these panes you can click on *Move Split* and then use the arrow keys on your keyboard to resize them either way. Figures 3.44 and 3.45 show the before and after when I used the Move Split tool to resize the slide deck thumbnails on the left side of the screen.

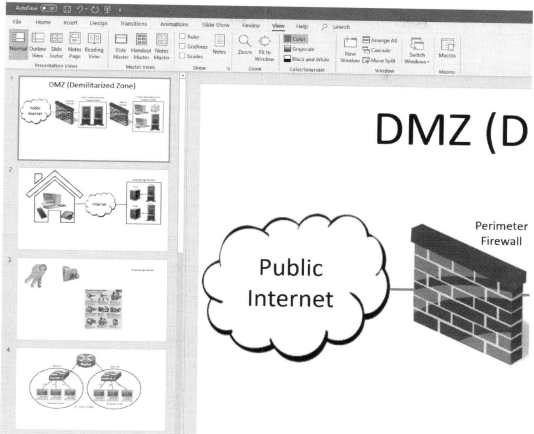

Figure 3.44

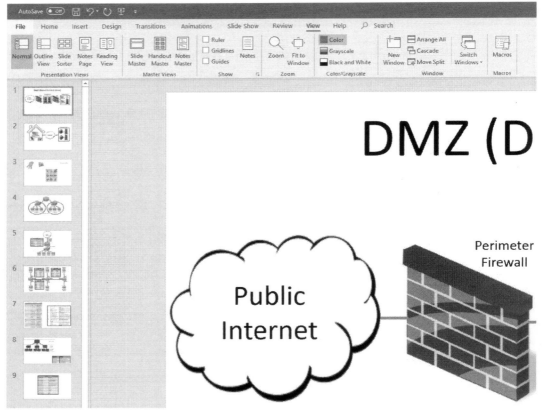

Figure 3.45

Macros

Macros are used as a time saving tool because they allow you to record a series of steps and then execute those steps by running the macro you created. They are also beyond the scope of this book!

Help Tab

I will just spend a little time on the Help tab because it should be obvious as to what it does. If you need help on how to do something within PowerPoint you can come to this tab and see if you can find what you are looking for. There is only one group here and it has several options within that group.

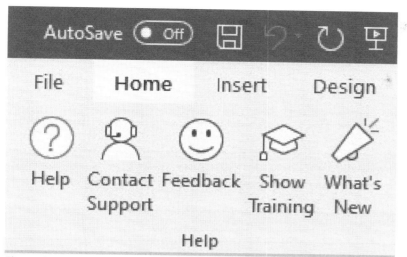

Figure 3.46

- **Help** – Here you can type in questions you are looking for an answer for or type in the name of a feature to see if you can find help to show you what it does or how to use it.

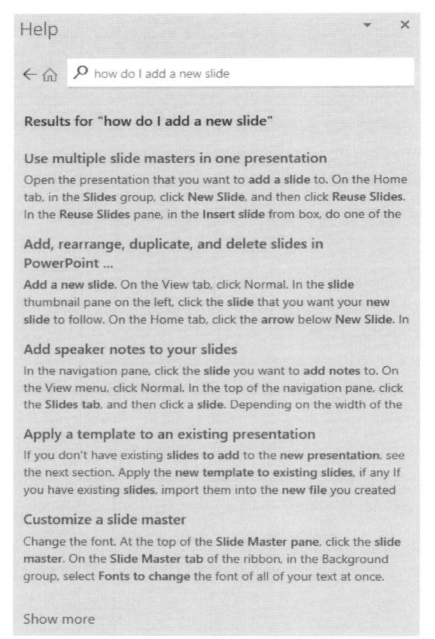

Figure 3.47

- **Contact Support** – This option is similar to the regular help option where you can type in what you want help with. The main difference is that it will bring up other support options that you can choose from such as a live chat. Just be careful when using this option so you don't end up paying for someone to answer a question for you.

- **Feedback** – If you want to voice your option and let Microsoft know what you think then you can leave some feedback or offer up a suggestion on how to improve their software. Your guess is as good as mine as to whether or not they really read these!

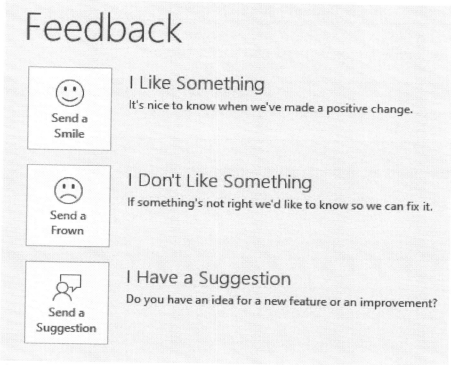

Figure 3.48

- **Show Training** – Microsoft offers some training resources that you can access right from PowerPoint itself. So if you feel like improving your skills even more than you will after reading this book you can see what they have to offer here.

Figure 3.49

What's New – When Microsoft introduces some new features to PowerPoint you can go to the What's New section and read up on these new additions to the software.

Chapter 4 - Creating a New Presentation

Now it's time to start working on a new presentation and getting our data added to it so we can format it and add some effects to it later. This is really where the fun begins because creating a presentation can kind of be like creating a work of art because you get to be creative and put your design skills to work! I will be covering formatting in the next chapter so this chapter will just focus on how to get your data into your presentation.

I often use PowerPoint to create graphics for my website and my books. It's very easy to move things around and resize them to make some professional looking graphics. Just remember the send to front and send to back options are your friends when using PowerPoint if you have things that overlap.

Choosing your Presentation Type

When you go to the File tab and click on *New*, you will be presented with the files that you have recently opened if you have any, or you might be shown some templates that you can use to get things started depending on your version of PowerPoint. If you don't see the templates right away then you can click on one of the suggestions or search for a specific theme or template that you can use to get started as shown in figure 4.2.

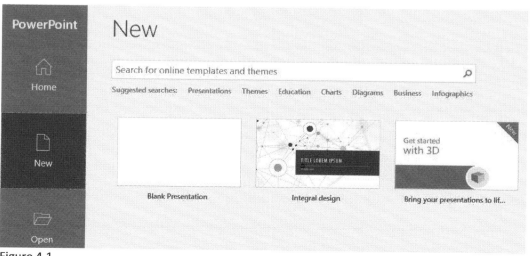

Figure 4.1

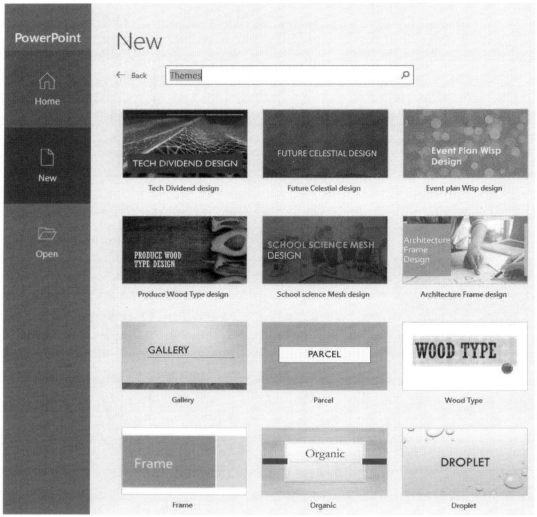

Figure 4.2

These themes and templates can be used to save yourself a bunch of work by adding colors and styles to your presentation for you. When you download a pre-configured presentation it will actually have the slides inserted and all you need to do is edit the text or any media you would like included in the presentation. Figure 4.3 shows an example of a preconfigured presentation file that you can use in PowerPoint.

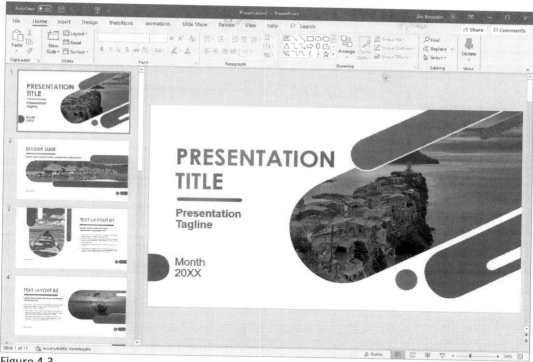

Figure 4.3

For this chapter, I am going to start from scratch and add some custom touches, so I will choose *Blank Presentation*. By default, PowerPoint blank presentations come with one slide and a text box for the slide title and another text box for the slide subtitle (figure 4.4). Other than that you essentially have a blank canvas that you can use to create your own completely personalized presentation with.

I will then add some additional slides to my presentation since I know I will be needing more than just the one slide that it comes with. To do so I can either go to the *Insert* tab and choose *New Slide* and pick the slide type I want or I can right click on a blank spot on the left where the slide deck is located and choose *New Slide* from there. If I choose the right click method it will insert a standard slide and won't give me the slide type choices that you will get when inserting a slide from the Insert menu.

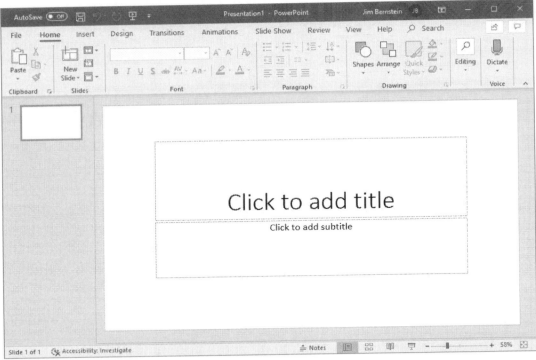

Figure 4.4

Inserting Text

A presentation without text is pretty much just a slideshow so it's important to add the right text to get your point across without overdoing it or making your slides hard to read. Inserting the text is the easy part, figuring out what you want to say can be the hard part.

Once you know what you want to put in your presentation all you will need to do is add a text box any type in your text or paste it in from another source such as an email or Word document etc. I sometimes like to remove the default title and subtitle boxes when creating a new presentation, but you can also use those as your initial text boxes if you like, just keep in mind that the text will retain the size of the title box unless you change it.

To add a text box, go to the *Insert* tab and then click on *Text Box* and use your mouse to draw a box about the size of the area you will want the text to go in. You should end up with something similar looking to figure 4.5. Don't worry about getting the size exact because you can easily reduce or enlarge the shape of the text box by clicking on one of the circles at the corners or side with your mouse and stretching it out or making it smaller.

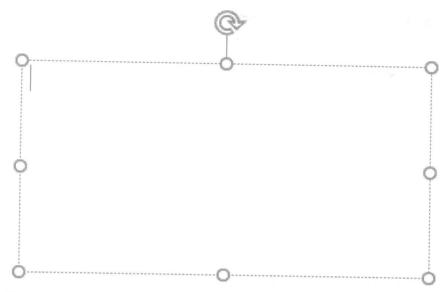

Figure 4.5

You might be wondering what the curved arrow is at the top of the text box. That is what you can click on to rotate the text box around to whatever position you like. Simply place your mouse over the curved arrow until it turns into a curved arrow and drag to the left or right to spin the text box.

Inside the text box, you will have a blinking cursor, and this is where your text will start once you start typing. If you don't have this cursor then you will need to click inside the text box to get it back. Then you can start typing just like you would in any other program on your computer and the text box will adjust its size automatically as you type.

You type your text inside of the text box and then you can format it later.

Figure 4.6

Once you have your text within the text box you can click on it and drag it anywhere you like within the slide. To do so, you will need to click on any edge/border of the text box and make sure the mouse pointer turns into a cross rather than clicking on the actual text itself.

Adding Images

Inserting pictures such as photos, drawings and clipart into your slides is a very widely used practice when it comes to making eye catching presentations. Adding images is just as easy as adding text and only takes a few steps. Once again this is done from the *Insert* tab and then the *Images* group. Before inserting an image you will need to decide what type you want to add.

I went over the various choices you have for the Images group in the last chapter so you should have a good idea of what each option will do. For my example I am going to insert a picture from my local computer's hard drive into my slide.

To begin I will click on the *Pictures* button and browse to the location on my hard drive that contains the picture I want to add. Then I can do things such as resize the image and move it anywhere I like on the screen. Figure 4.7 shows that I now have my text box and my image on the same slide. Notice how when the image is selected the box around the text disappears? That is because the box will only be shown on the selected item, so you know which object you are working with. Also notice that the box around the image extends over too far on the left and right side? I will fix this later when I get to the chapter on formatting.

You type your text inside of
the text box and then you
can format it later.

Figure 4.7

If you have a newer version of PowerPoint you might have noticed that it will offer up Design Ideas (figure 4.8) when you place an image or other items into your presentation. If you like any of their ideas then you can click on it and have it applied to your slide.

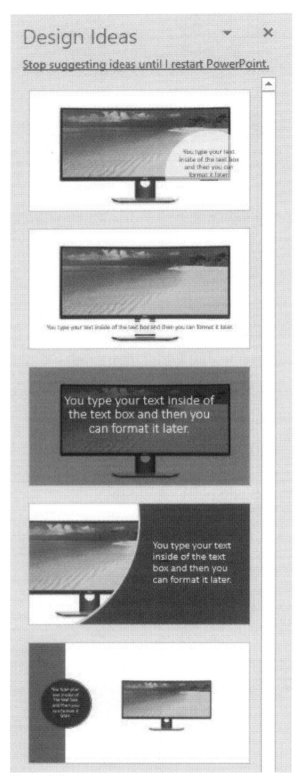

Figure 4.8

Adding Audio and Video

If you have something like a video or audio clip that goes along with your presentation then they can be added just like you would text and images. When inserting a video you can either add one from your local computer and place it within your PowerPoint file which can take up a lot of space or you can embed an online video into your presentation and just have it stream from the Internet during your show.

Keep in mind that the more pictures and videos etc. you insert into your presentation, the larger your PowerPoint file will be. So if you are planning on emailing your file you might run into a case where its too large and have to find another way to get it to its destination like sharing it via Dropbox or other cloud storage service.

I will be embedding a video from YouTube into my slide so that way I don't need to add the actual video file to my presentation. To do this I go to the Insert tab once again and then to the *Media* group. Next, I will click on *Video* and choose *Online Video.* From here I will need to enter the URL (address) for the video I want to add to my presentation. The easiest way to do is to go to the video I want to add online and then just copy the address and paste it in the box as shown in figure 4.9.

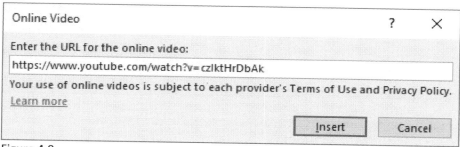

Figure 4.9

Now I have my YouTube video place on my slide next to the text and image that I added earlier. Once again I can drag the video anywhere I like on the slide and even resize it to make it fit better with the existing content on the page. Notice how the video overlaps the image and cuts off the bottom of the monitor? I will show you how to adjust that as well in the next chapter on formatting.

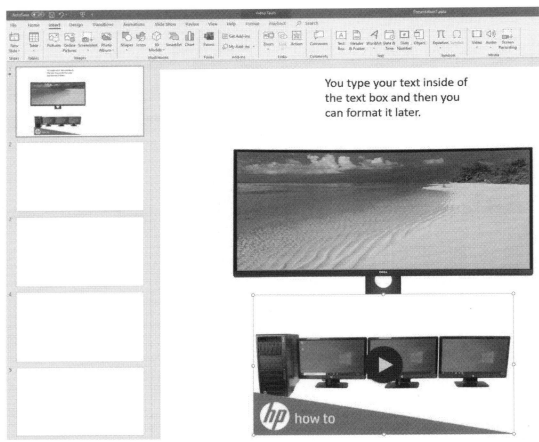

Figure 4.10

After you have inserted your video into PowerPoint you can actually click on the play button and watch the video right from the slide editing mode to make sure it plays correctly.

Figure 4.11

If you want to insert a video that you have on your computer then it's done the same way as if you were inserting a photo that you have stored on your hard drive.

Adding audio is similar to adding images and video and it's just a matter of either adding a sound file from your local computer (such as an MP3 or WAV file) or recording audio from your microphone and having it added to your computer. Once you have your audio place you will have a speaker looking icon with audio controls such as play, forward, reverse and volume (figure 4.12).

Figure 4.12

If you choose to record your own sound then you will see a record dialog box where you can press the record button and then give it a name when you are finished. Then you will see another speaker icon in your presentation that represents your newly recording audio.

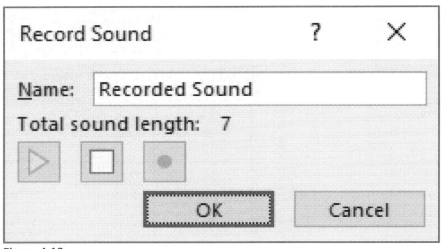

Figure 4.13

Inserting Shapes and Other Illustrations

Since the main reason for creating a presentation is to share information or provide training to others it's very common to use things such as shapes, icons and charts into your slides to help get your point across. Fortunately there are many upon many ways to do this in PowerPoint.

Some of the more commonly used objects to insert into a PowerPoint presentation are shapes, especially lines, arrows and boxes. If you click on the *Shapes* button in the *Illustrations* group you will see that there are many shapes to choose from and they are categorized making it easier to find what you are looking for.

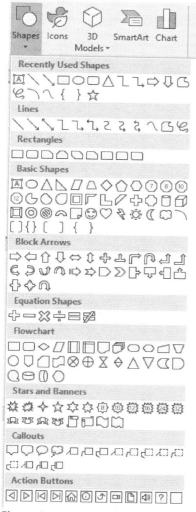

Figure 4.14

Let's say I want to have an arrow connecting my video to my audio file. All I need to do is choose the type of arrow I like and then draw it where I want it to go. Then I can format it to change the way it looks if needed. If you take a look at figure 4.15

you will notice that it has the same options to resize and rotate it as the other objects I inserted did.

Here is an example of what it should sound like.

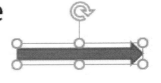

Figure 4.15

Inserting an *icon* works the exact same way and once you insert one you can manipulate it just like you can with shapes.

SmartArt consists of premade graphics that represent things such as hierarchies or relationships between items and this might not be an area you will use too often if ever. You can scroll through the various categories to see what kind of SmartArt is available to use.

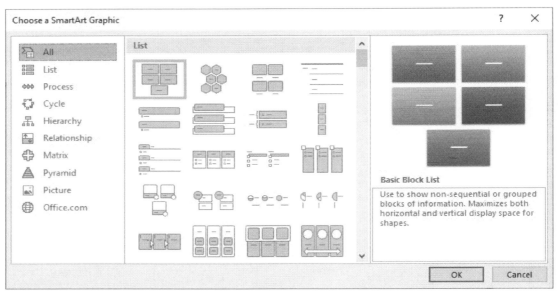

Figure 4.16

For example, I can create a pyramid graphic and fill in the text any way I like as shown in figures 4.17 and 4.18.

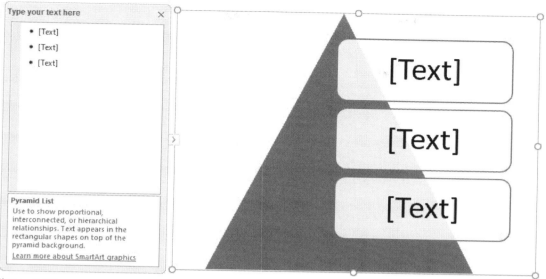

Figure 4.17

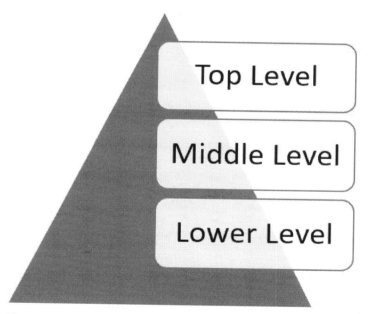

Figure 4.18

Charts, on the other hand, are more commonly used and are a great way to show how your data sets relate to one another. There are many types of charts you can choose from such as the good old fashioned column, line, pie and bar charts as well as more complex types of charts such as radar and histogram.

When you select a chart type you will see the various options for that type of chart that you have to choose from. Figure 4.19 shows what options I have for a column type of chart.

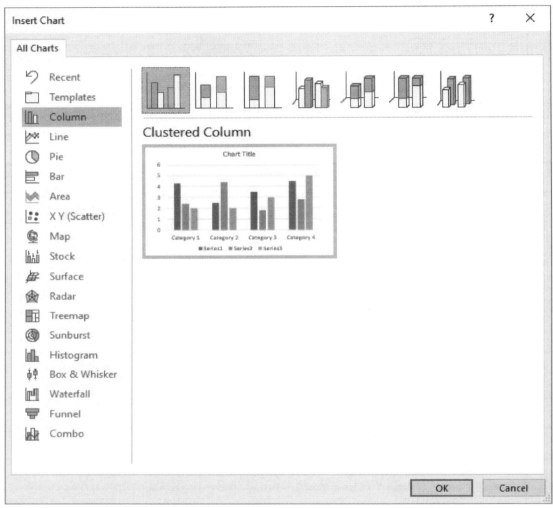

Figure 4.19

After I choose my chart type it will be inserted into my slide along with an Excel type spreadsheet where I can enter in my data (figure 4.20). Then all I need to do is change the information in the spreadsheet and my chart will update itself with the new information as seen in figure 4.21.

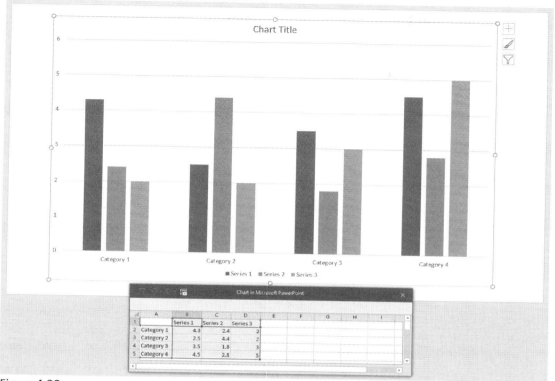

Figure 4.20

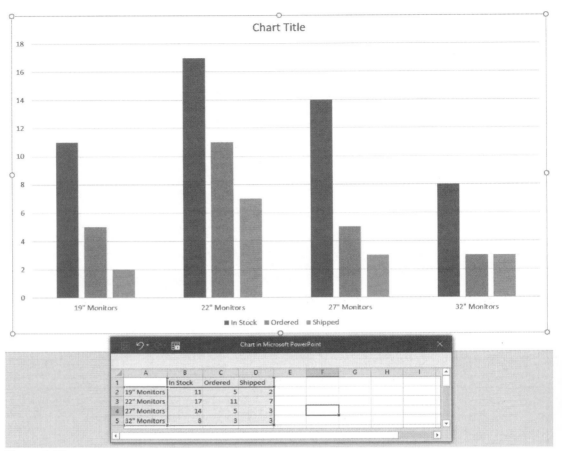

Figure 4.21

At the top right of the chart, you will see some buttons that you can click on that will let you edit various aspects of your chart. The + button will let you enable or disable various chart elements such as axis titles, chart titles and gridlines.

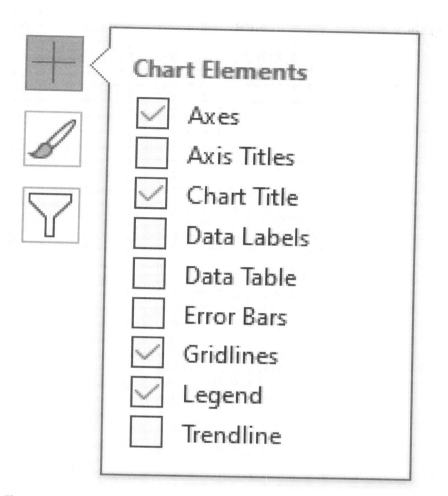

Figure 4.22

The *paintbrush* button will allow you to change the style and color of the chart.

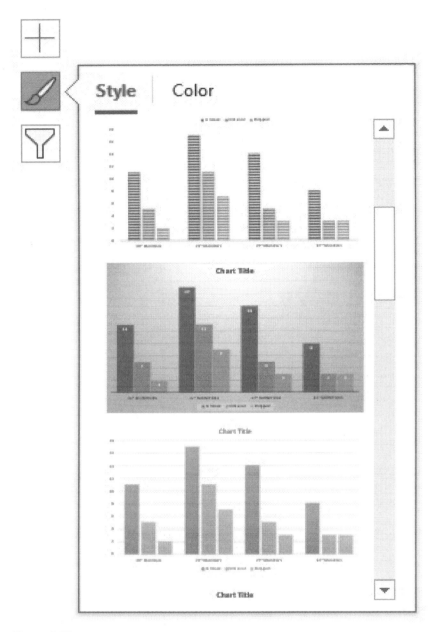

Figure 4.23

Finally, the *filter* button will let you change various values and names that your chart contains as well as show or hide them.

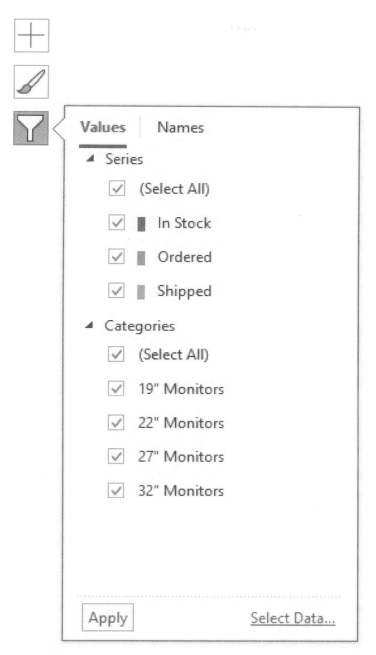

Figure 4.24

Copying, Moving and Deleting Slides

I mentioned how to insert a new slide into your presentation in the last chapter but to refresh your memory you can do so from the Insert menu or by right clicking on the slide deck where you want the slide to go and choosing *New Slide*. You will

91

most likely run into a situation where you will need to copy, move or delete a slide and that is just as easy as adding a new one.

Copying a slide

There is more than one way to copy a slide depending on what you are trying to accomplish. If you want to copy the slide itself and then just paste it into your slide deck as an additional slide then you have a few options. One of the more common ways is to right click on the slide and choose *Copy*. Then you can right click where you want the slide to go and under the *Paste Options* you will have three choices.

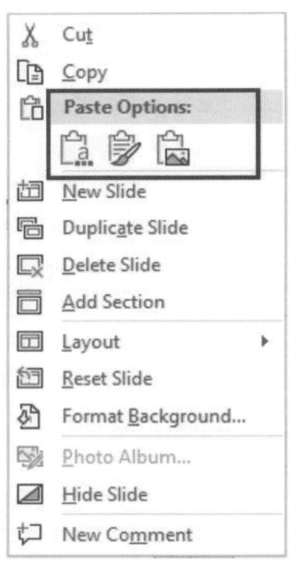

Figure 4.25

- **Use Destination Theme** – This will paste in a copy of the slide and apply the theme that is being used where you are pasting the slide at.

- **Keep Source Formatting** – This will paste in a copy of the slide and keep all the formatting of the slide rather than change it to match the formatting of where you are pasting the slide.

- **Picture** – This option will paste the contents of your slide into another slide as an image or screenshot rather than an actual slide that you can work on.

Another option you can use to copy your slide is the *Duplicate* feature. This will make a duplicate copy of your slide right under the position of the current slide. To use this feature make sure you have the slide you want to duplicate selected and then you can right click on it and choose *Duplicate*. You can also do this from the *Copy* drop down arrow in the *Clipboard* group on the *Home* tab.

When using PowerPoint or pretty much any software for that matter, right clicking can be used to quickly perform common tasks. Depending on where you right click, the menu options will change to reflect things you can do from that particular area of the program. Give it a try while working on your presentation and see how it works!

Moving a Slide

Moving a slide is similar to copying a slide except you are you won't have two copies when you are done but instead are moving the slide from one place to another. The process works the same but instead of using the Copy option when right clicking on your slide, you will use the *Cut* option. Then you can use the same Paste Options as you would for copying a slide.

A quick and easy way to move a slide is to simply drag it where you would like it to go in the slide deck. All you need to do is click and drag the slide from one position to the other and then release the mouse when you have it where you want it to be.

Deleting a Slide

When you have some content that you want to remove you can either delete all of the objects on your slide to have it be a blank slide once again or you can simply just delete the slide itself which is a much easier way to accomplish this.

To delete a slide simply select the slide that you want to remove from the slide deck on the left and then press the delete key on your keyboard. Or you can right click on the slide and choose *Delete Slide*. If you want to delete multiple slides then you can hold down the Ctrl key (Command on a Mac) or Shift key and highlight the slides you want and then delete them.

Chapter 5 - Formatting Your Presentation

Once you get all of the information you need into your presentation you can then format everything to make it look more presentable and give it that wow factor that will keep people's attention while you are showing your presentation. Of course you can format things as you go along if you would rather do it that way and some people actually prefer to use this method.

This chapter will be focusing on how to format things such as text, images, themes and so on in order to make everything fit together. Since PowerPoint is all about the visuals, it's important to make things look like they fit together. One thing I want you to keep in mind is that I am not going to end up with a fancy professional looking presentation after going over my examples but rather just show you what you need to do in order to get a professional looking presentation.

Themes
Themes are used to add colors, designs and typestyle changes to your slides making it easy to "spruce" things up without having to make a lot of manual changes on your part. There are many built in themes to choose from within PowerPoint and if you don't like the ones that come with the program then you can download many more from the Microsoft website. (https://templates.office.com/).

Themes can be found on the Design tab and all you need to do is find one you like and then click on it to have it applied to your presentation (figure 5.1). For my example, I will use the first one on the list which is a basic shaded green theme since is fairly simple and won't make things look too cluttered.

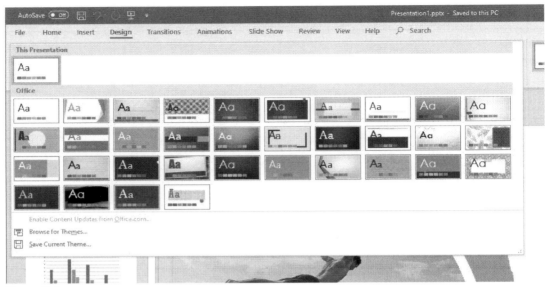

Figure 5.1

Figure 5.2 shows my main slide and slide deck before the theme is applied and figure 5.3 shows how everything looks after the theme has been applied.

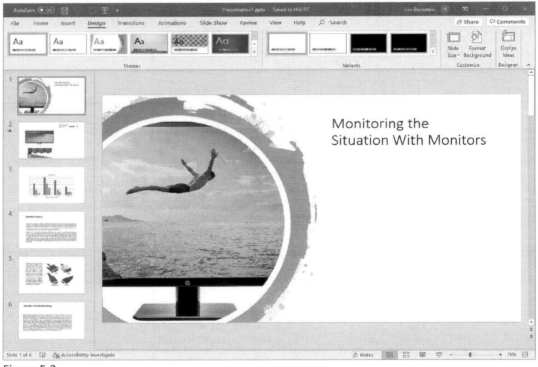

Figure 5.2

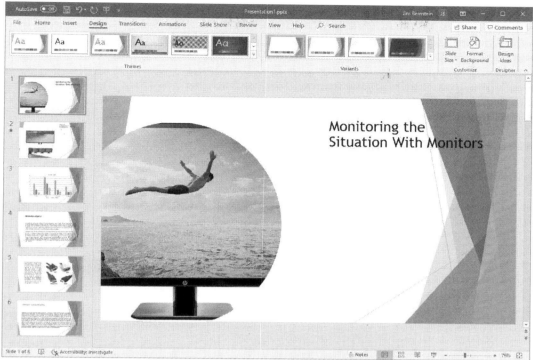

Figure 5.3

This theme also changed the colors of the bars in my chart on slide 3 to match the theme so when you apply a theme to your slides make sure to check and see if it changed anything you didn't want to be changed.

If you look to the right of the *Themes* group there is the *Variants* group which allows you to choose a different version of the same theme where the colors can be different, and where you can also change other aspects of the theme such as the fonts and background styles (figure 5.4).

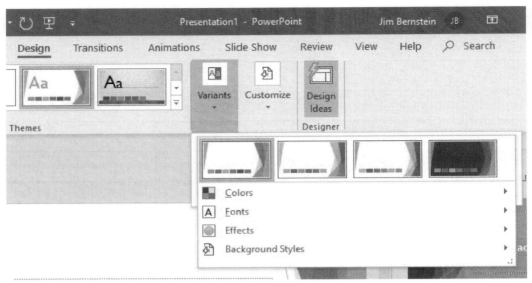

Figure 5.4

Slide Master

Before getting too far into our topic of formatting, I wanted to take a minute to go over the Slide Master and what it does. If you plan to create many slides that will be using the same font, colors, layouts, company logo and so on you don't want to have to make all of these changes on every slide whenever you create a new one. This is where the Slide Master comes into play and it allows you to make changes on one slide and have those changes apply to some or all of your other slides. To get to the Slide Master, click on the *View* tab and then on *Slide Master* in the *Master Views* group. After you do so, you will see a new tab called Slide Master and will also notice that your slide and slide deck changes as seen in figure 5.5.

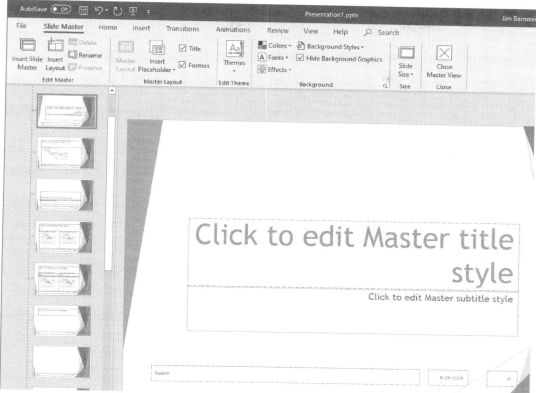

Figure 5.5

When in Master Slide view, the slides in your slide deck represent various types of slides that you can have in your presentation such as the Master Slide, Title Slide Layout, Section Header Layout and so on (figure 5.6). Each one of these types of slides can be edited so changes to these slides will be applied to all other slides of this type. For our conversation, we will just be focusing on the Master title slide at the top and once you get down how the process works, you can experiment with the other slide types.

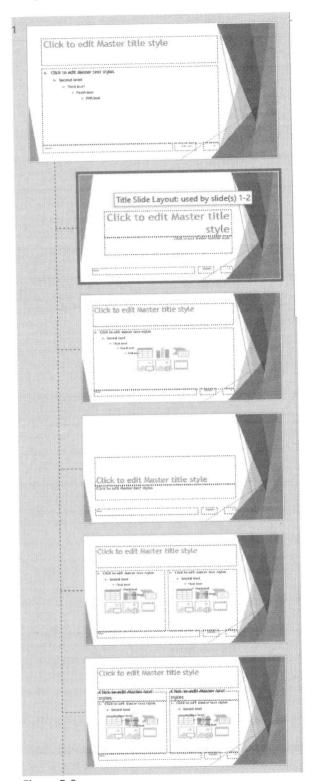

Figure 5.6

When you click on the main Master title slide at the top, you will be able to edit how things will look for all of your slides since changes made to this slide will apply to all other slides while changes to other master slide types will only apply to certain slides.

So now that we got that down (I hope), let's make some changes to the Master title slide and see how they apply to all of the other slides. Here is a listing of all the changes I will be making. Once I make these changes on the Master title slide only I will click on the *Close Master View* button.

- Change the title font to Broadway and make it larger
- Make the body font italicized
- Add a smiley face to the lower right of the slide
- Add a light grey background

Figure 5.7 shows the results of the changes I made to the master slide. You can compare it with figure 5.3 which shows how the slides looked before the changes.

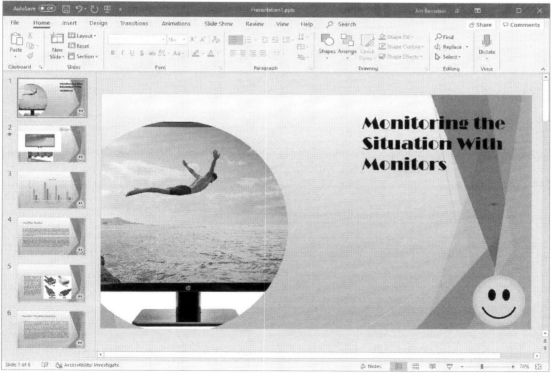

Figure 5.7

Using the Slide Master view takes a little bit of practice (and patience) to get the hang of it so you can use it effectively so take your time with it and be sure to check out the changes you make to make sure things look the way you want them to look.

Formatting Text and Images

Formatting text and images in PowerPoint is pretty much the same as formatting them in Microsoft Word or most other office type software. So if you are a proficient Word user then you should be able to format your text and pictures in PowerPoint with ease.

Formatting Text

There isn't much to the process of formatting text as long as you know where to go to find the formatting options. And once again, right clicking is your friend when it comes to formatting options. And of course you can use the formatting options from the Home tab as seen below which is what most people do.

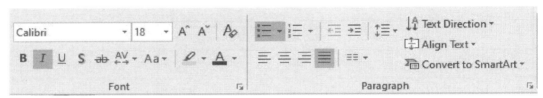
Figure 5.8

To format your text all you need to do is highlight the text you want to change and then choose how you want to change it. For my example, I want to change a couple of words from my last slide to make them bold and also change the text color. So to begin with I will highlight the words I want to change with my mouse as shown in figure 5.9.

Monitors do and will go bad at some point, so it's important to make sure that when your screen starts showing psychedelic colors or simply nothing at all, you make sure it's the monitor itself rather than the computer or even the cable. You can start by checking the connections on the monitor and on the computer to make sure they are secure and not loose. Next you can try to replace the cable with another one, or even try flexing the cable down the entire length of it to check for shorts. If the image on the monitor changes as you bend the cable, then you are most likely looking at a bad cable. If your monitor has more than one connection type, such as VGA and HDMI, you can try that type of connection (assuming your computer has the matching connection type). Finally, if everything looks good, you can connect your monitor to a different computer or laptop and see if it works or not. If it does the same thing there, then you can assume it's bad. If it works on a different computer, then you are looking at a video card or motherboard issue on your computer, and that might involve taking it in to be looked at by a professional.

Figure 5.9

Then I can go up to the Home menu and choose the *B* for bold and then the *A* with the colored bar underneath it to change my text color. If you hover your mouse over a particular button\icon in the toolbar, it will tell you what that button does.

I can get the same editing options (and more) by right clicking anywhere on the text that I have highlighted.

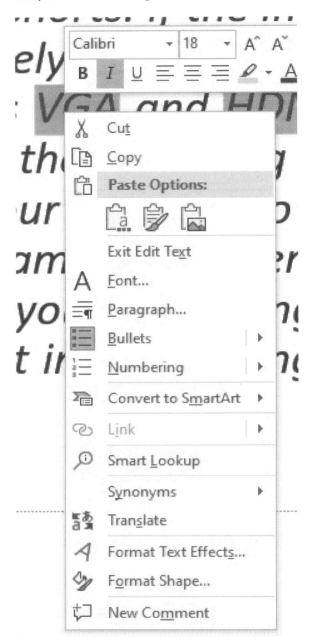

Figure 5.10

If you are aware that you can use the Shift key to select contiguous files on your computer and the Ctrl key to select non-contiguous files then you might be interested to know that the same applies with text. So if you want to highlight 2 or more words that are not next to each other you can hold down the Ctrl key while highlighting them one at a time.

One thing you may have noticed when you highlighted text is that a new tab named *Format* showed up in the Ribbon. Here you will find some additional formatting options such as adding WordArt or Alt Text to help people with visual impairments read your text.

Figure 5.11

To summarize, all you really need to know about editing text is how to highlight the text properly and then where to find the right tool to make the changes you need. I suggest going back to the Home tab section in Chapter 3 if you need to refresh your memory on what tools do what. I will be getting into more details on what the Format tab does as I go along in this chapter.

Formatting Images

Getting your pictures to look right on your slides is a pretty easy task but there are also some custom touches you can add to them to really make them stand out. You might remember that I had a picture of a monitor on one of my slides that covered part of my video as well as part of my text as well. If you look closely at figure 5.12 you will see that there is some extra white space in the monitor image that is the cause of my problem.

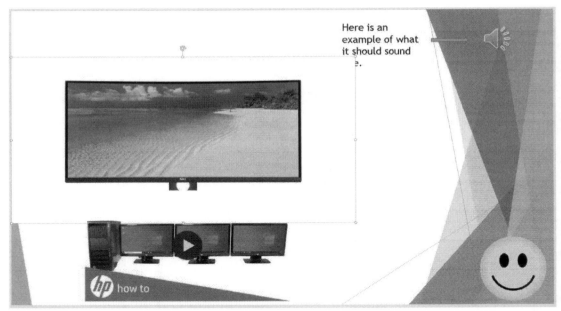

Figure 5.12

I'm going to begin by cropping the monitor image to get rid of that extra white space. If I double click the image it will bring up the Format tab on the Ribbon where I can choose the *Crop* option from the *Size* group.

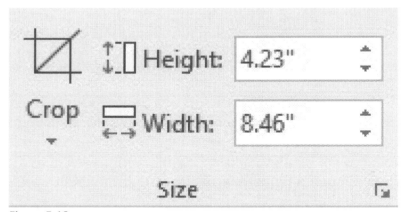

Figure 5.13

When I click on Crop it will make some black "handles" on each corner as well as on each side of the image as shown in figures 5.14 and 5.15.

Figure 5.14

Figure 5.15

What you need to do is click and hold on any one of the handles to drag in the area you wish to crop. The corners will move the crop area in from two directions while the side or top handles will bring the crop area in from just one direction. The dark area in figure 5.16 shows what part of the image will be cropped out and the lighter area shows what you will be left with. Figure 5.17 shows the finished result.

Figure 5.16

Figure 5.17

If you look closely, you will see that we still have a problem because the bottom half of the monitor is cut off, or at least appears to be cut off. What is really happening is that the how-to video is sitting on top of the monitor. This is an easy fix that I will be discussing in the next section but before I get there I want to go over some other image formatting options you can use.

There are many other tools that are available when you "activate" the Format tab by double clicking on a picture and I will now go over those options to you have an idea what each one of them does.

Figure 5.18

Corrections

Here you can do things such as adjust the brightness and contrast as well as sharpen and soften your images. There are some built in presets that you can use, or you can fine tune these settings yourself individually.

Color

If you don't like the color of your picture you can use some of the built in color correction options for saturation and tone. You can also have PowerPoint change the coloring of your picture completely using one of the built in presets.

Artistic Effects

PowerPoint comes with many built in effects to help make your images stand out and give your presentation a more custom look. You can even create your custom effects from the Artistic Effects Options. Figure 5.19 shows an example of a cutout effect.

Figure 5.19

Transparency

If you want your image to have a faded out look or want to use it behind some text and make sure the image doesn't overpower the text, then you can add a level of transparency to your picture. You can choose one of the preset levels or create your own custom level of transparency.

Picture Styles

Picture Styles are used to add some flare to your images and give them a custom look that would normally require you to use some fancy photo editing software to achieve. You can click on any of the built in styles to see how they apply to your picture until you find the one you want. Figure 5.20 shows an example of one of these styles.

Figure 5.20

Picture Border
Many pictures tend to look better when they have a border around them because they will stand out more and PowerPoint makes it easy to create simple borders for your pictures. When creating a border you can choose your own line weight, dash type and color.

Figure 5.21

Picture Effects
Another fun way to make your pictures stand out is to apply a Picture Effect to them. There are many built in effects to choose from such as shadows, reflections, glow and 3D rotation as shown in figure 5.22.

Figure 5.22

Picture Layout

You might not ever have a need to use the Picture Layout feature of PowerPoint, but I want to take a moment to go over it just in case. This feature allows you to apply a custom image and text layout to an existing image in case you want to apply some text to your picture. When you select a picture on your slide and then choose one of the layout options as seen in figure 5.23 it will then apply that layout to your image. An example can be seen in figure 5.24.

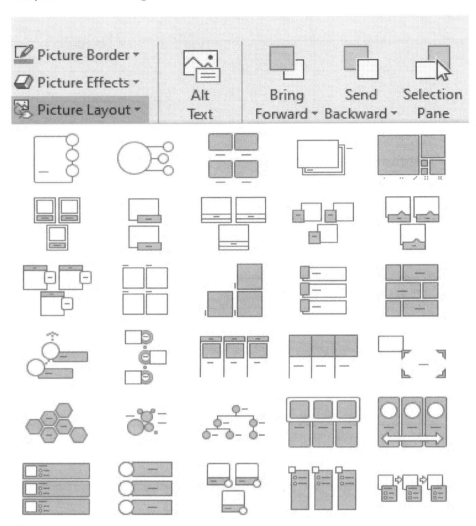

Figure 5.23

Figure 5.24

Arranging and Aligning Your Objects

Continuing our conversation from earlier in the chapter where my monitor picture was being partially covered by my video as seen once again in figure 5.25, obviously we don't want our slide to look this way. Fortunately, this is an easy fix and it only takes a couple of clicks to get things looking right.

Figure 5.25

There are two ways I can fix my overlapping problem from figure 5.25. I can either bring the monitor image forward so it's not behind the video or send the video backward behind the monitor image. Keep in mind that using either method will not always work for these types of situations and you might only be able to use one of the options depending on the circumstances.

In this case, I am going to bring my monitor image forward to it's not behind the video. To do this I can go to the *Arrange* option in the Drawing group on the Home tab (figure 5.26). I can also get to this from the Arrange group on the Format tab (figure 5.27).

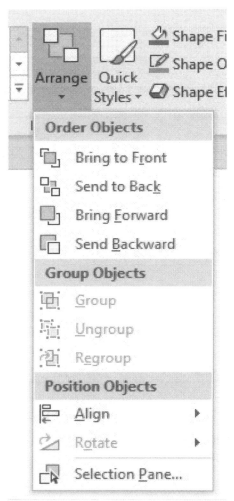

Figure 5.26

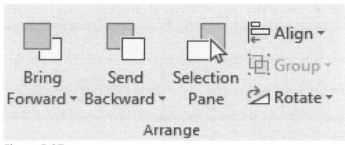

Figure 5.27

116

And of course you can always right click on your picture and get similar options from there.

Before I make this change I want to mention the *Selection Pane* option as seen in figure 5.27. Using this tool you can see the order (levels) of all of your objects within your slide. Then you can do things like move them forward or backward compared to other objects or even hide them by clicking on the eye image next to the object.

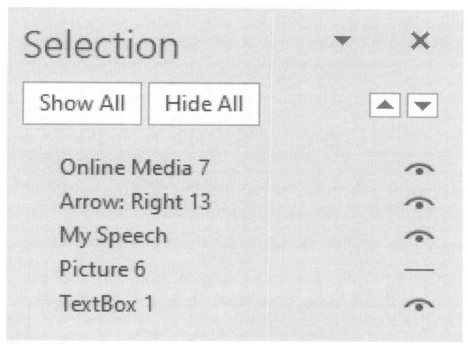

Figure 5.28

Now back to the matter at hand. I will now click on my monitor image and choose the *Bring Forward* option to have it brought forward one level. I can do this as many times as I need until it is brought all the way to the front of all the objects if that is my goal. Or I can just use the *Bring to Front* option to have it brought all the way to the front (top level) in one click. Figure 5.29 shows the results and you can see the video is not blocking the monitor image anymore. This process also works for objects such as text boxes, charts, sound files and so on.

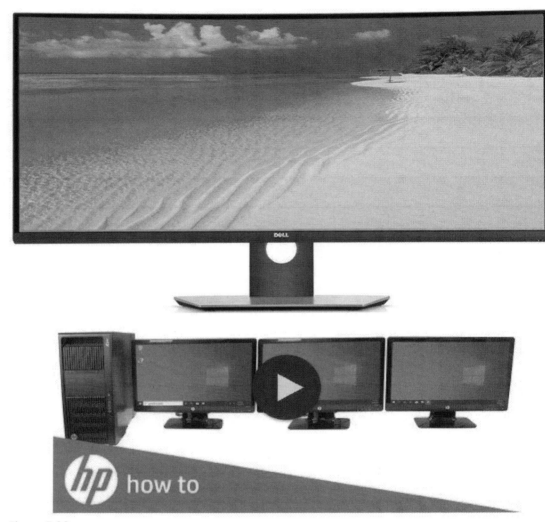

Figure 5.29

 One way to get around the problem of the extra "white space" that many images have around them that fills in the extra space to make the rectangular image is to use transparent PNG files. These PNG files don't have the extra white space around the picture. This requires a little photo editing on your part to make your images transparent, but I just wanted to mention it.

Alignment Options

You probably know by now that you can align the text on a page or in a text box by making it left justified, right justified and centered, etc. and the same thing applies to objects on your slides. I personally think its easier to just drag and drop my objects where I want them to be on the page but if you want things to line up precisely then you can use one of the alignment options as shown in figure 5.30.

Figure 5.30

Under the Align option, you will see the *Rotate* tool which will let you rotate your images clockwise or counterclockwise as well as flip them horizontally and vertically. Figure 5.31 shows an example of the same image with one of them being flipped horizontally.

Figure 5.31

Changing the Slide Background

If using a theme seems like a little overkill for you then you might want to try changing the background of your slides to spruce them up instead. The Format Background tool can be found on the *Design* tab in the *Customize* group. Here you

120

will have several options to choose from to format your background in a variety of ways.

You can use a solid color, gradient fill, add a picture or texture or use a pattern fill. You can also change the transparency of your new background in case it ends up overpowering your text and graphics and you want to lighten it up a bit.

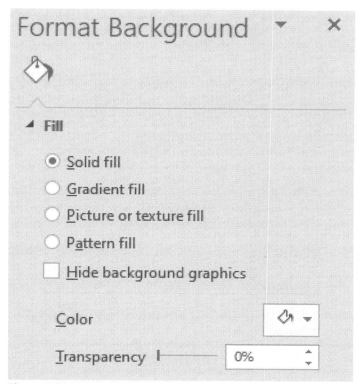

Figure 5.32

Figures 5.33 through 5.36 show some examples of the types of background fills you can apply in PowerPoint.

Gradient Fill

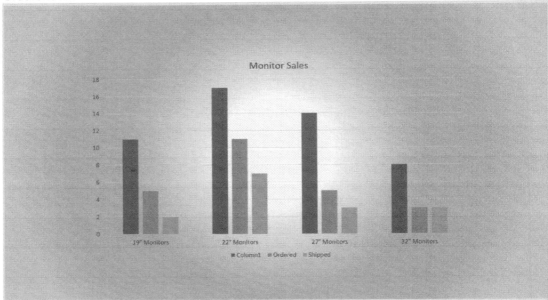

Figure 5.33

Texture Fill

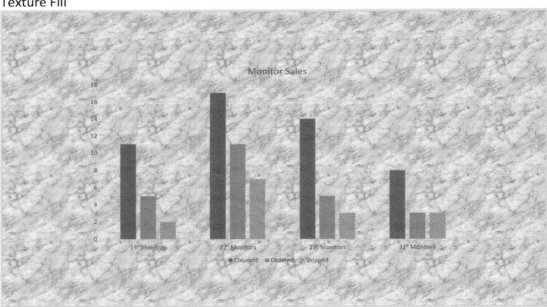

Figure 5.34

Picture Fill

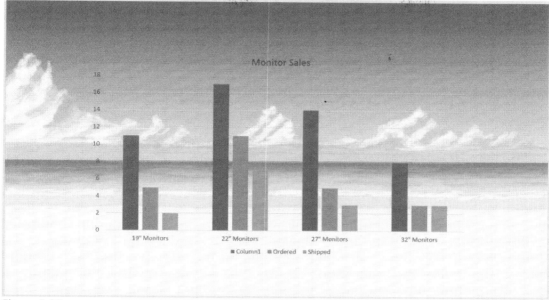

Figure 5.35

Pattern Fill

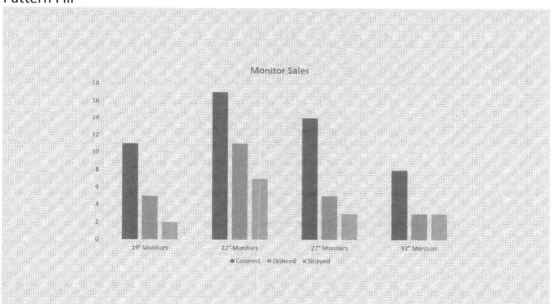

Figure 5.36

Formatting Shapes

Adding shapes to your slides is a very common thing to do and most of the time the default shape formatting won't apply to the look you are going for. When you add a shape to a slide, PowerPoint adds its own fill, color line width and so on. If you are using a theme with a certain color, PowerPoint will match that color when you add a new shape, but this might not be the look you are going for which means you will need to format your shape.

Double clicking on the shape will bring up the Format tab where you will have some options for changing the way your shape looks (figure 5.37) but I prefer to right click on my shape and choose *Format Shape* to get the options as shown in figure 5.38.

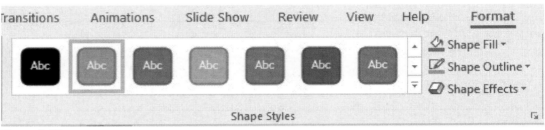

Figure 5.37

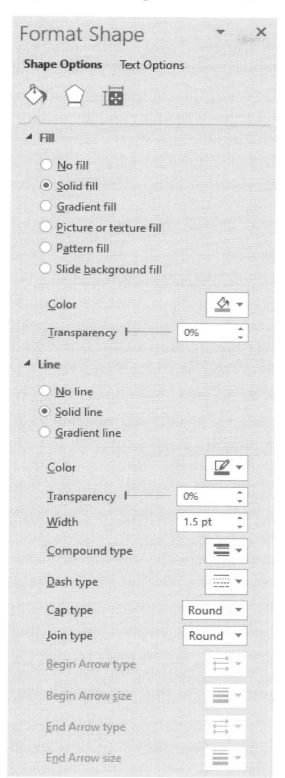

Figure 5.38

From here you can do things such as change the type of fill, the fill color or remove it completely. You can do this same thing for the line of the shape and if you remove the fill AND the line your shape will be technically invisible, so you don't want to do that! The *Transparency* option will make the shape lighter and give a see-through effect.

You can also change the width of the line and also it's compound type which I prefer to call the line style. Cap type and Join types are only used with certain kinds of shapes so if you choose a different type and it doesn't change anything then you will know why. For example, here is a line with a round cap and then the same line with a square cap.

Figure 5.39

The arrow type and size settings only apply to arrow shapes that are found in the Line category and not block arrows for some reason.

Slide Numbers & Date and Time
To me, side numbers in a presentation are more for the presenter than for the audience since people don't read a presentation like a book. One of the main reasons for page numbers is to use them for reference or for notes. They also come in handy if you are planning on printing out your slideshow to give to your audience as a handout.

Adding slide numbers is an easy process and works in a similar way to adding a footer into a Word document. To perform this process, go to the *Insert* tab and then click on the *Slide Number* icon in the *Text* group. When you do this it will bring up the same settings box as if you were to click on *Header & Footer* or *Date & Time*.

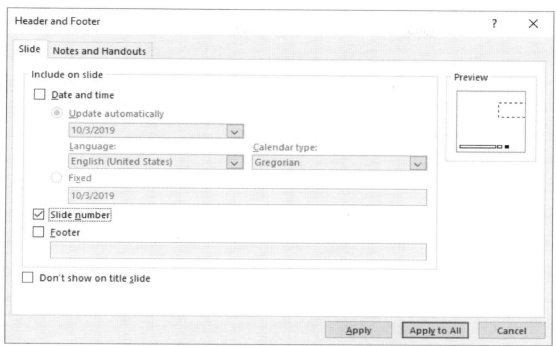

Figure 5.40

Next, you will check the box for Slide number and click on *Apply* to have a page number added to just the slide you are on or *Apply to All* to have page numbers added to all of your slides. Some people don't like to have a page number on the first (title) page so if that's the case, check the box at the bottom that says *Don't show on title slide*. Depending on if you are using a theme or not will determine where the page number is placed and its color etc. For my presentation, it added the page number outside of the theme graphic and also made the page number text color match the theme color (green in my case).

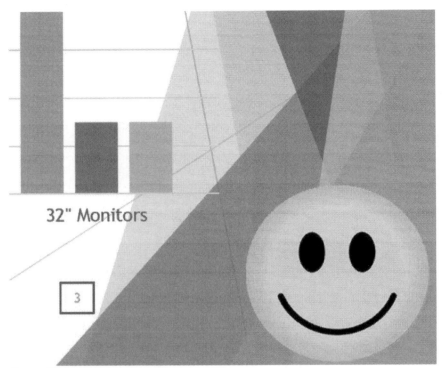

Figure 5.41

If for some reason you want your audience to know the current date and time or have a specific date and time shown on your slide, you can do this from the same screen as seen in figure 5.40. If you choose the *Update automatically* option then the date and time will adjust itself each time you show or open the presentation. There are several date and time formats you can choose from if you click on the arrow to bring up the format list. The *Fixed* option will use whatever date you enter in there and keep that date the same no matter what day it is.

Chapter 6 - Using Transitions and Animations

What makes presentation software so special and different from just showing a bunch of pages from your word processor program is the ability to add transitions and animations to your slides to give it the wow factor that will hopefully keep your audience awake just in case your content is putting them to sleep!

Some people get transitions and animations confused or think that they are the same thing, but they are not. When it comes to transitions and animations you can use both of them, or just one of them within your presentation. This is an important chapter, but it will still be a short one. The best way to learn how to use transitions and animations is to play around with them and see firsthand how they work. I will now go over each one individually.

Transitions

Transitions are effects that you can apply to your slides, but these are used in between slides rather than on your slides. You will find these on the Transition tab and PowerPoint has many built-in transitions you can choose from. If you don't use transitions, when you advance to the next slide it will just simply appear after you click the mouse button rather than do something like slide or fade in.

You choose your transitions from the *Transition to This Slide* group as seen in figure 6.1 and 6.2. As you can see, there are many types to choose from so it shouldn't be hard to find one that suits your style.

Figure 6.1

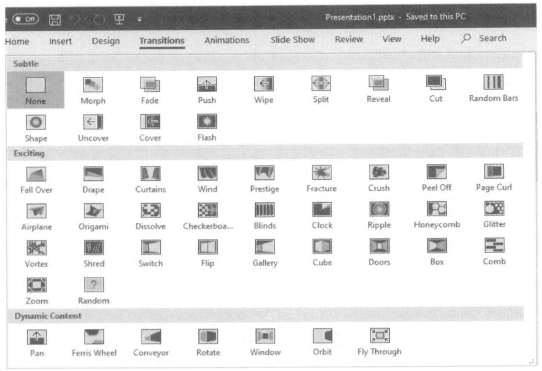

Figure 6.2

When applying a transition make sure that you are on the slide that you want the transition to apply to. So if you want the effect to happen between slides 3 and 4 then make sure you are on slide 4 when adding the transition. Once you apply the transition, PowerPoint should show you a preview of how it will look. To see it again, simply click on the *Preview* button in the Ribbon.

After you choose your transition and effects options, you then need to decide if it will apply only to the slide you have selected (the default), or if you want to have that transition apply to *all* the slides. If you want it to apply to all the slides simply click the *Apply to All button* in the Timing group (figure 6.3).

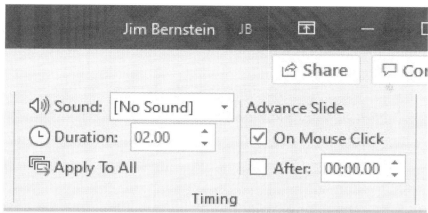

Figure 6.3

The *Duration* setting will determine how long the transition takes to apply and move to the next slide. Of course, I can't show you a demonstration since this is a book and all, but it's very easy to play around with transitions on your own.

If for some reason you want there to be a sound that plays when you switch to the next slide then you can choose one from the *Sound* drop down or choose a custom sound file that you have stored on your computer. The *Loop Until Next Sound* option in the Sound dropdown list will make the sound repeat itself during your slideshow until you go to the next slide.

Most people like to have control over when the next slide appears on the screen and to do that you should leave the box that says *On Mouse Click* checked so the presentation will stay on the current slide until you click your mouse to move on to the next one. If you want a more hands free approach then you can check the box that says *After* and put in a specific time that the slide will stay on the screen before it automatically advances to the next one.

One thing you will notice as you add transitions and animations to your slides is that there will be a small star to the left of the slide in the slide deck indicating that there is some type of animation present on that slide as shown next to slide 2 in figure 6.4.

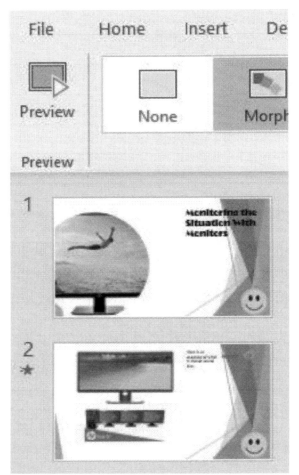

Figure 6.4

Animations

Animations are similar to transitions, but you apply them to objects within your slide rather than the slide itself. So you can have multiple animations for your objects on a slide but just one transition between slides. Animations are what you use within your slides to make custom effects and control how your presentation moves along. They can be used to have text, images, charts, etc. appear on command with the click of the mouse. They can do things like slide in or appear out of thin air, and you can choose what order all of your animations happen in.

When you go to the Animations tab you will notice that it looks similar to the Transition tab and that there are many animations to choose from (figures 6.5 and 6.6).

Figure 6.5

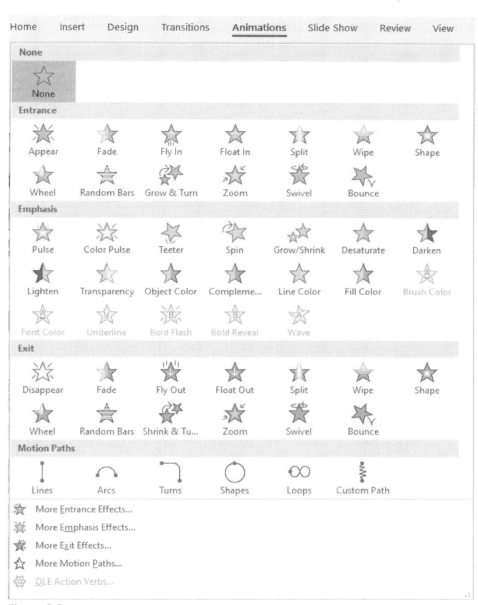

Figure 6.6

Down at the bottom of figure 6.6 you will also see that there are even more animations you can check out from each category and here is what the animations from each category are used for.

- **Entrance** – These are commonly used for objects that make an entrance on the slide. For example, if you have some text describing a particular thing and then want to have the picture of that thing appear or fly onto the slide after the text.

- **Emphasis** – These are used to highlight an object on your slide to make it stand out. For example, you can use the Grow/Shrink animation to have a picture grow in size right on the slide to help make your point.

- **Exit** – When you are done talking about a particular object you can use an Exit animation to have it leave the screen.

- **Motion Paths** – These can be used to make an object move in a certain path determined by you. Once you choose a path you can then edit that path to have the object move exactly the way you like, or you can create a custom path from scratch. For example, figure 6.7 shows that I applied a diamond path to an image. The image will move along that diamond shaped path but if I want to edit that path, all I need to do is drag the diamond to change its shape/path. It works in a similar fashion to editing a shape that you would add to a slide.

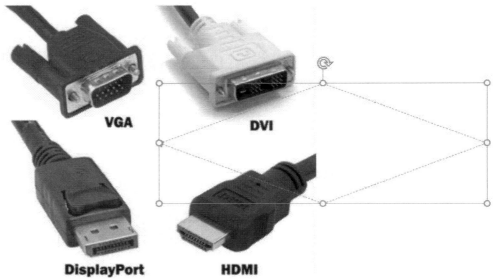

Figure 6.7

To create an animation for an object, select the item you want it to apply to and then click the *Animations* tab.

The Animations tab has the same *Effect Options* button as the Transition tab, and the options will vary based on what animation you choose. There is also a *Duration* setting like the transitions have, and also a *Delay* setting in case you don't want the animation to happen immediately.

The *Reorder Animation* setting under the *Timing* group will let you change the order of the animations that you have applied. To use this feature simply click the object that you have applied the animation to and then choose either *Move Earlier* or *Move Later* from that setting.

To fine tune your animations you can adjust the settings from the *Start* option. Here you can determine when the animation takes place. Many people just leave the default setting of *On Click*, but you can also have it take place after a different animation finishes, as well as with or after the previous animation.

You can use the *Animation Pane* in the *Advanced Animation* group to see your animations and to change their order, as well as change other settings such as their timing and effect options. Once again, if you right click on an animation you get a menu that gives you quick access to some of the configuration options.

Figure 6.8

When you are all ready to go remember that there is the Preview button at the left of the Ribbon that will play your slideshow within the PowerPoint window. It will play the animations automatically, so you don't have to actually click through each one. Pressing F5 on the keyboard will start the presentation in slide show mode full screen and allow you to click through it as if you were actually giving the presentation.

When using transitions and animations, it's crucial to use the Preview button after each change to make sure things are in the proper order and that they make sense when you actually show your presentation.

Chapter 7 – Saving, Showing, Sharing and Exporting Your Presentation

Now that you have your presentation looking exactly the way you want it to with all the transitions and animations in place, it's now time to show it to the world. Or maybe just your coworkers for now!

In order to make use of your presentation and have all of your hard work pay off, you will need to make your presentation available for others to see and there are several ways to do this depending on your goals. For example, you might be planning on showing it directly from your laptop to a projector or maybe you need to send it to someone in another state for them to approve or maybe modify. In this chapter, I will be going over various ways to save, show and share your presentation.

Saving Your Presentation

When you save your presentation, it will be saved as a *.pptx* file which is the default file type for PowerPoint files. File extensions are used by the operating system (Windows, Mac, etc.) to tell it what program to use to open a particular file type. So if you just save your presentation as *MyPresentation.pptx* then when you double click on that file, your computer will open it using PowerPoint. If you make up your own file extension or remove it then your computer won't know what to do with the file so make sure you don't change it. Sometimes your operating system will hide certain file extensions so you might not even see it even though it's really there.

PowerPoint presentations can be saved as other types of files as well and there are cases when you might need to save your presentation as a different kind of file. If you go to the *File* tab and then click on *Save as,* and then click on the drop down arrow next to the Save button you will see that there are many different types of files that you can save your presentation as (figure 7.1). You will see that PowerPoint Presentation (*.pptx) is the default file type. Even though are many other types of files that you can save your presentation as, you will most likely not use many of the other choices.

Figure 7.1

One type that you might end up using is the *PowerPoint Show (.ppsx)* which saves your file as a slideshow that can only be played, and not edited or changed. This is commonly used when you want to send your presentation so someone and only let them have the ability to show it as a slideshow when they open the file. When you save your presentation as a ppsx file, it will even change the way the icon looks to represent a projector screen compared to the normal file icon as seen in figure 7.2.

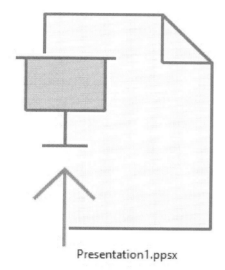 

Presentation1.ppsx   Presentation1.pptx

Figure 7.2

Now I would like to take a moment to go over some of the other file types that you might use just so you have an idea of what types of files you can save your presentation as.

- **PowerPoint 97-2003 Presentation** – If for some reason you know someone who is using a very old version PowerPoint (pre-PowerPoint 2007) and they need to be able to work on your file then you can save it using this version.

- **PDF** – Portable Document Format files are very common and are a great way to send your presentation in a smaller sized file while making where the person on the other end is not able to edit your presentation. They will not be able to open the file with PowerPoint ether.

- **PowerPoint Template** – If you spent a lot of time designing a presentation and want to be able to use this design for other files then you can save it as a template file that you can open and edit for new presentations. Just be sure to use the default template file location of your computer so you can easily access it later. Then when you go to create a new presentation it will be shown under your Personal templates and you can choose it to base your new presentation on.

- **MPEG-4 or Windows Media Video** – Presentations can be saved as video files that can then be played on pretty much any computer or device that supports common video file types such as MPEG movies etc. It will take a bit of time to save the file as a video and there will be a status bar at the bottom of the screen showing the progress (figure 7.3). Once you are done you can open the file with your video player and watch the slideshow that way (figure 7.4).

Figure 7.3

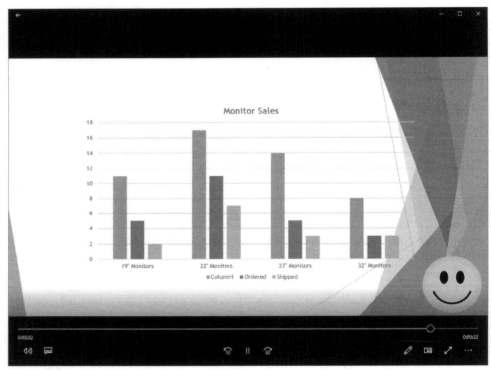

Figure 7.4

- **GIF, JPEG, PNG or TIFF** – Saving your presentation as an image file allows you to have one or all of your slides converted to that image type making it easy to send someone just one slide or let someone see your presentation without needing to open it in PowerPoint. You can also use this for other things such as posting one of your slides on your website or even making it the background image on your computer. Figure 7.5 shows all the separate JPG files that were created when I saved my presentation as an image.

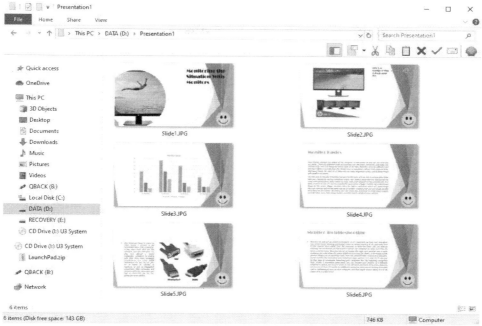

Figure 7.5

Exporting Your Presentation

When you export a presentation, it is similar to saving as a different type of file in some respects but then again it's not... if that makes sense! The Export options are also listed under the File tab just like the Save As options and figure 7.6 shows you what you have to work with.

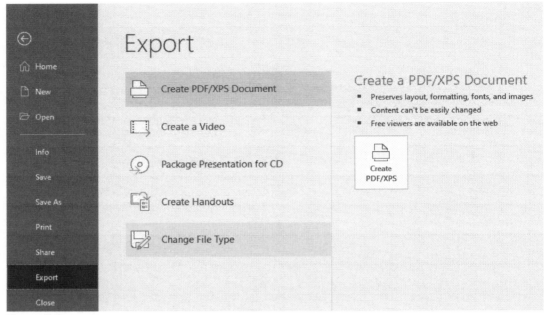

Figure 7.6

I discussed exporting to a PDF in the previous section and an XPS Document is Microsoft's version of a PDF file and works the same way.

The Create a Video option is similar to the Save As video option except when you do it from the Export section you get some additional options. You can do things such as change the resolution from standard to Ultra HD (4K) if you are going to be showing it on a high resolution projector or monitor for example. You also have options as to whether or not to use any narrations you recorded or custom slide timings you have setup.

Create a Video

Save your presentation as a video that you can burn to a disc, upload to the web, or email
- Includes all recorded timings, narrations, ink strokes, and laser pointer gestures
- Preserves animations, transitions, and media

⊘ Get help burning your slide show video to DVD or uploading it to the web

| Full HD (1080p) |
| Large file size and full high quality (1920 x 1080) |

| Use Recorded Timings and Narrations |
| Slides without timings will use the default duration (set below). This option includes ink and laser pointer gestures. |

Seconds spent on each slide: 05.00

Create Video

Figure 7.7

The *Package Presentation for CD* option comes in handy if you want to have your presentation put together with all the needed files to make it show properly in one place and then burn it to a CD. Then you can give this CD out to others and they can watch it on almost any computer without needing to have PowerPoint installed.

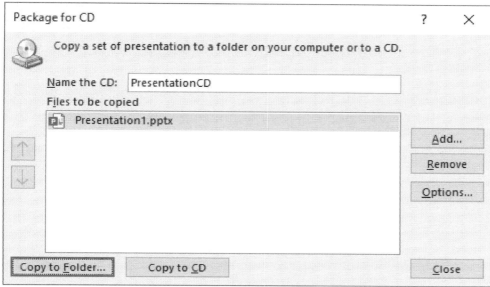

Figure 7.8

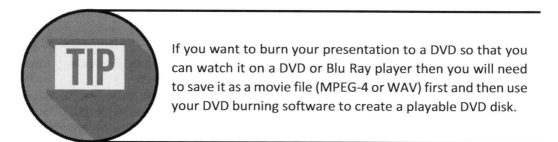

If you want to burn your presentation to a DVD so that you can watch it on a DVD or Blu Ray player then you will need to save it as a movie file (MPEG-4 or WAV) first and then use your DVD burning software to create a playable DVD disk.

Many people like to print out handouts to pass around to their audience so they can follow along and take notes during the presentation. The *Create Handouts* option allows you to easily export your slides into Microsoft Word to create various types of handouts that can then be printed out (figure 7.9).

When you chose the Create Handouts option you have several layout choices to choose from. For example, if you have notes for your slides you can have them printed out next to the slides or you can have blank lines printed out next to the slides as shown in figure 7.10.

The *Paste link* option automatically updates the Word document with any changes to the slides. This comes in handy if you are making a lot of changes and need to have your handouts updated each time to reflect those changes.

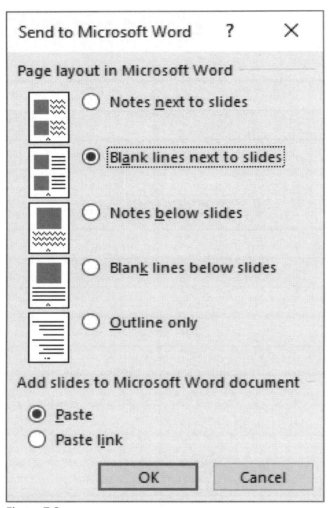

Figure 7.9

Figure 7.10

The final Export option is called *Change File Type* and is very similar to the Save As option that I previously discussed. In fact, there is even a Save As button at the bottom of the Change File Type interface making it easy to choose additional file types to save your presentation as.

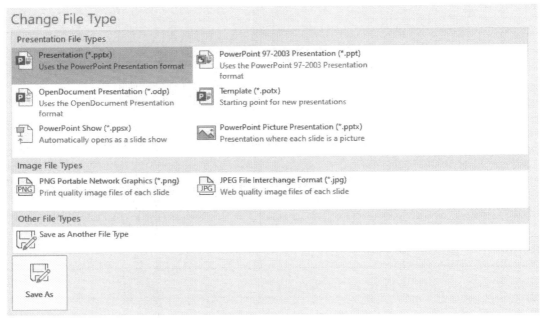

Figure 7.11

Running a Slideshow

The main reason anyone creates a PowerPoint presentation is to eventually show their work to an audience as a slideshow. This audience might be your coworkers in the office, or you could have even made a presentation about your vacation full of pictures that you can show your friends and family.

Whatever your reason for creating a presentation may be, you need to know how to present it smoothly, so it looks like you know what you are doing! Running a slideshow is a fairly easy thing to do and it's always a good idea to practice it first to make sure things are looking the way you planned for them to be and that all of your transitions and animations are correct.

The easiest way to start your slideshow is to click on the projector screen icon on the Quick Launch bar. You can also press the F5 key on your keyboard to start the slideshow as well.

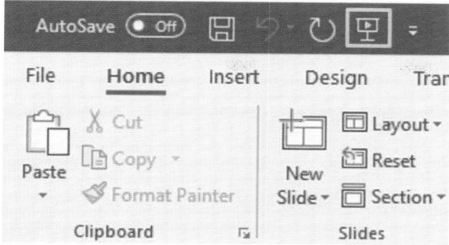

Figure 7.12

You might remember that there is a *Slide Show* tab that has a couple of ways for you to start your show as well.

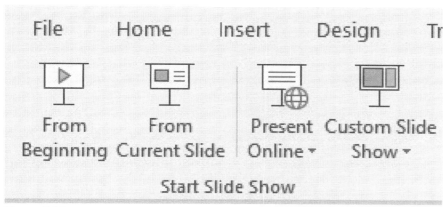

Figure 7.13

During the slideshow, you can use things such as your mouse to advance to your next slide as well as the right arrow key on your keyboard. Then you can use the left arrow to go back a slide. You can also use the up and down arrow keys to go back and forth as well.

While presenting your slideshow you can right click on any slide to get additional options as shown in figure 7.14.

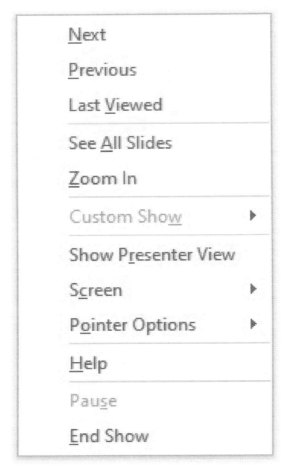

Figure 7.14

Most of these choices should be obvious as to what they do but I want to go over a few that might not be so obvious.

See All Slides
When you choose this mode, you will get a screen that only you can see that will show all the slides in your presentation making it easy to jump to a different slide without having to scroll through all of the other slides.

Figure 7.15

Zoom In

If you need to show a closeup view of something on your slide or emphasize something on the screen you can use the Zoom In option to enlarge that part of the screen. When you click on Zoom In you will see a lighter colored box and your mouse cursor will turn into a magnifying glass and then you can choose where you want to zoom into and simply click the mouse to have that section enlarged.

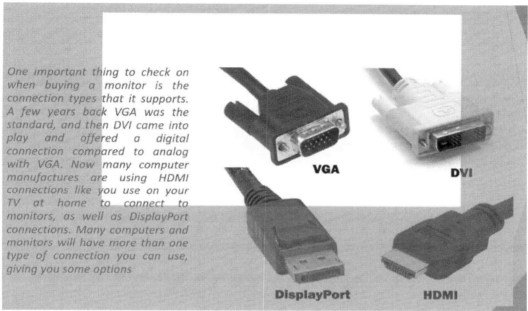

One important thing to check on when buying a monitor is the connection types that it supports. A few years back VGA was the standard, and then DVI came into play and offered a digital connection compared to analog with VGA. Now many computer manufactures are using HDMI connections like you use on your TV at home to connect to monitors, as well as DisplayPort connections. Many computers and monitors will have more than one type of connection you can use, giving you some options

Figure 7.16

Show Presenter View

Presenter View (figure 7.17) is used to help you navigate your slideshow without the ones you are presenting it to seeing what you are up to. It will show the main slide that is currently being shown on the left of the screen and then show the next slide that is coming up on the right hand side of the screen. Then next to the slide it will show any notes that you have made for the current slide in case you forgot what you were going to say! You will also see additional options such as blacking out a slide or zooming into a slide etc.

Figure 7.17

Screen

If you want to get your audience to focus on you rather than what is on the screen then you can use the Screen option to either have the screen go completely black or white. Then all you need to do is click with your mouse to have the slide come back on again.

Pointer Options

Here you can use various tools such as a pen or highlighter to make notes or emphasize certain areas of your slide by drawing on it (figure 7.18). There is even an eraser if you make a mistake and need to correct something. When you exit this mode you will be asked if you want to keep your markups or not on your slide. If you choose not to then your slide will go back to the way it was when you exit this mode.

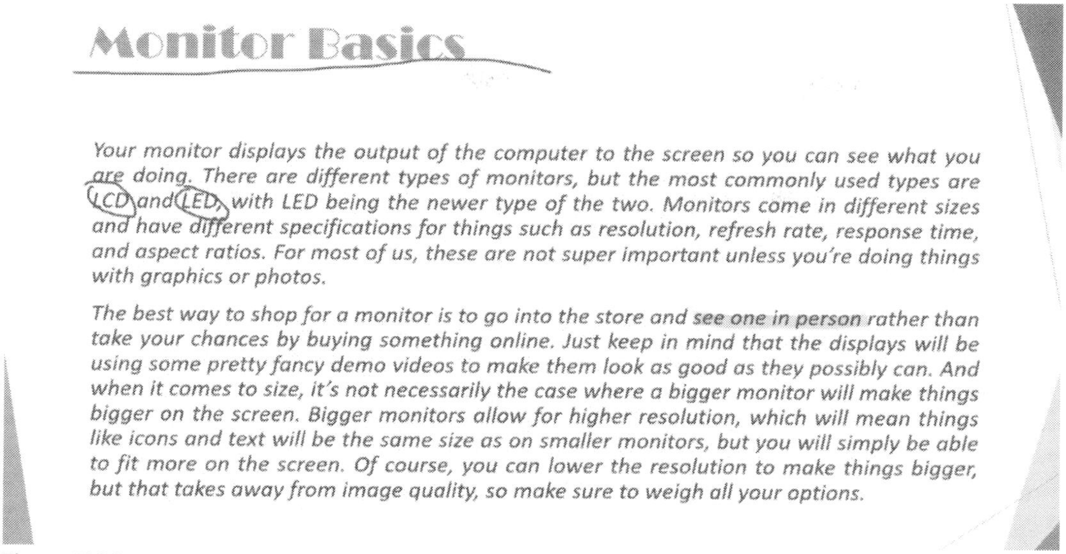

Monitor Basics

Your monitor displays the output of the computer to the screen so you can see what you are doing. There are different types of monitors, but the most commonly used types are LCD and LED, with LED being the newer type of the two. Monitors come in different sizes and have different specifications for things such as resolution, refresh rate, response time, and aspect ratios. For most of us, these are not super important unless you're doing things with graphics or photos.

The best way to shop for a monitor is to go into the store and see one in person rather than take your chances by buying something online. Just keep in mind that the displays will be using some pretty fancy demo videos to make them look as good as they possibly can. And when it comes to size, it's not necessarily the case where a bigger monitor will make things bigger on the screen. Bigger monitors allow for higher resolution, which will mean things like icons and text will be the same size as on smaller monitors, but you will simply be able to fit more on the screen. Of course, you can lower the resolution to make things bigger, but that takes away from image quality, so make sure to weigh all your options.

Figure 7.18

I mentioned that you can start your slideshow with the F5 key, and I would also like to show you some other handy keyboard shortcuts that you might find useful when using PowerPoint. Keep in mind these shortcuts are for Windows users although some will apply to Mac users as well.

Function	Keyboard Shortcut
Start a presentation from the beginning	F5
Start a presentation from the current slide	Shift+F5
Start the presentation in Presenter View	Alt+F5
Hide the pointer and navigation buttons	Ctrl+H
Stop or restart an automatic presentation	S
End the presentation	Esc
Go to a specific slide	Type the slide number, then press Enter

View the All Slides dialog	Ctrl+S
Return to the first slide	Home
Go to the last slide	End
Stop media playback	Alt+Q
Play or pause media	Alt+P or Ctrl+Space depending on your version
Mute the sound	Alt+U

Sharing Your Presentation with Others

Collaboration is a big thing when it comes to how businesses operate these days and there is an increasing need to be able to quickly and easily share information in order to increase productivity and keep things running smoothly.

PowerPoint provides you with an easy way to share your presentations with others which makes it easy for them to either show it to people on their end or make changes of their own for your team. This is all done via the Internet and cloud storage such as Microsoft's OneDrive online storage service.

OneDrive is free to use for anyone who has a Microsoft account or who wants to sign up for one. The free account gives you a limited amount of online (cloud) storage that you can use to upload and share any types of files you desire. If you need additional space or advanced features then you can subscribe to one of their monthly plans for an additional cost.

To share your presentation you first need to get it uploaded to your OneDrive account. You can do this manually via the OneDrive website or OneDrive app if you have it installed on your computer. Or you can go to the File tab and then *Share* and the first time you share your presentation you will be prompted to upload it to your OneDrive account as shown in figure 7.19. From here you will also have the ability to simply attach it to an email as a PowerPoint file or PDF file.

Figure 7.19

When you choose the OneDrive share method you will be prompted to add the email address or addresses of the people you want to share it with. You can also decide if they can only view the file or if they can edit it as well. Finally, you can add a personal message that will get sent to them along with the invitation.

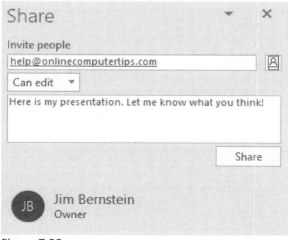

Figure 7.20

Once you share the file you will see that the email address or addresses of the people who have access to it will be listed under the Share invitation section.

Figure 7.21

Figure 7.22 shows an example of what the invitation will look like that the person on the other end will receive in their email.

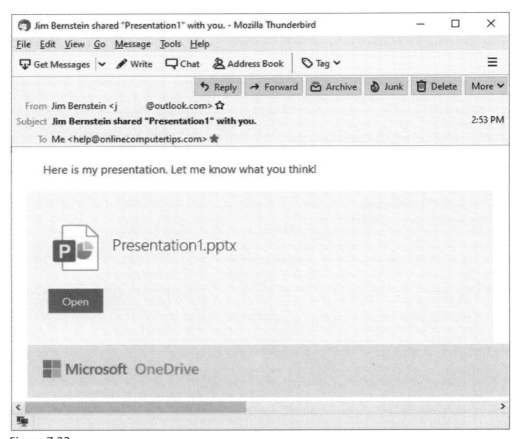

Figure 7.22

When they click on Open in the email, the PowerPoint file will open using Office Online which allows you to view and work on Microsoft Office files via a web browser. If you have a subscription to Office 365, then it will most likely use that to open the file. Figure 7.23 shows how my presentation looks when opened up in the Google Chrome web browser. It looks very similar to when I open it up on my computer but there are not as many editing options when using Office Online.

Figure 7.23

When someone works on your presentation online and makes changes, those changes will be saved to the file and you will see the changes the next time you open up the online version. Any changes they make to the online version will not affect the file you have saved on your local computer so be aware of which file you are working on when you have copies online and on your hard drive!

Chapter 8 - Printing Your Presentation

By now you realize that PowerPoint presentations are meant to be shown on a projector or on a large screen of some sort rather than be printed out on paper. But this doesn't mean there won't ever be a need for you to print out your masterpiece on paper to give to someone else or maybe post on the wall in the conference room.

Printing your presentation is a fairly simple thing to do and there are only a few adjustments you can make when printing it out so this chapter will be nice and quick. It will also be the last chapter and I'm sure you are glad to get it over with right?

Choosing a Printer and Changing Printer Options

Just like with anything you print, you will need to make sure you are printing it to the correct printer if you have more than one and then you should check the printer settings to make sure it's set to print the way you want it to print.

When you go to the File tab and then click on Print you will see a print settings page similar to figure 8.1. There are two main sections in this area, and they are *Printer* and *Settings*. PowerPoint will print to your computer's default printer if you don't change it to a different printer from the dropdown printer selection, assuming you have another printer installed to choose from.

There is a link named *Printer Properties* underneath the printer choice and that is where you can go to change printer specific settings.

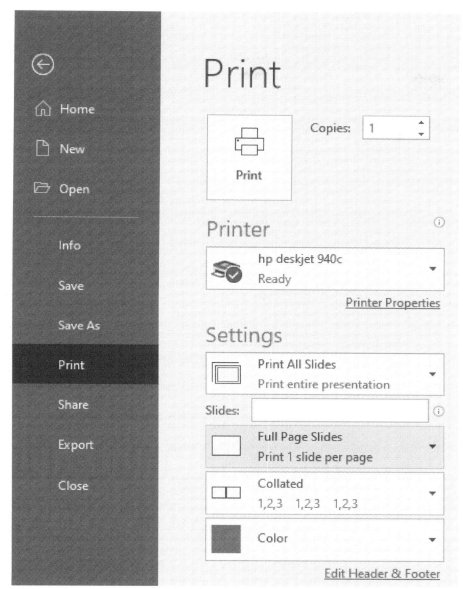

Figure 8.1

Figures 8.2 and 8.3 show some common printer settings such as layout configuration (portrait and landscape) and page printing order. You can also do things such as tell PowerPoint what printer tray to use and what quality to use for printing. The settings here will vary depending on what printer you are using.

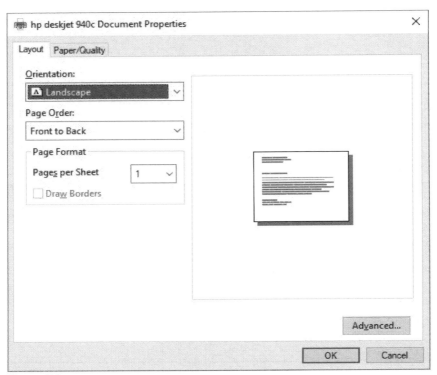

Figure 8.2

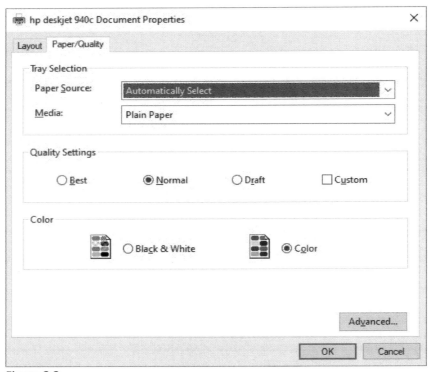

Figure 8.3

Changing Presentation Printing Options

There are multiple ways to print out your presentation in PowerPoint and the way you choose will most likely depend on how your presentation is formatted and how you want it to come out on paper. When you go to the print options area right under Settings you will see that you have several ways to print your slide.

- **Print All Slides** – This will obviously print out all the slides within your presentation.

- **Print Selection** – With this choice, you can highlight specific slides in the slide deck and then go to Print Selection and it will only print out the slides that you have selected.

- **Print Current Slide** – This will print out the slide that you are currently on. So if you are looking at slide 3 and choose this option, then only slide 3 will be printed out.

- **Print Custom Range** – Here you can type in specific slide numbers that you want to print such as **2-5** or **1-3, 5, 8** which will print out slides 1 through 3 and also slides 5 and 8.

The next print option allows you to print using specific layouts or handouts. Under the *Print Layout* section (figure 8.4) you can choose from the following.

- **Full Page Slides** – This will print out the slide to look just like it does within PowerPoint. Just make sure to choose the landscape print option to make it fit correctly on the page if you are using the default settings.

- **Notes Pages** – If you added any notes to your slides this will print out a smaller image of the slide with your notes underneath.

- **Outline** – This option will print your slideshow out in an outline format. It will only print out the text so if your slides are mostly images or shapes, it might not do you much good.

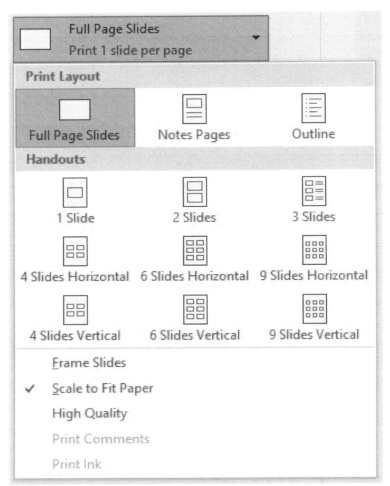

Figure 8.4

I have discussed printing your handouts in the last chapter and from the *Handouts* section you can choose how many slides to print on a page and whether to print them horizontally or vertically on the page.

The Frame Slides option will put a thin frame around the slide itself that will appear when you print it giving it a more polished look as seen in figure 8.5.

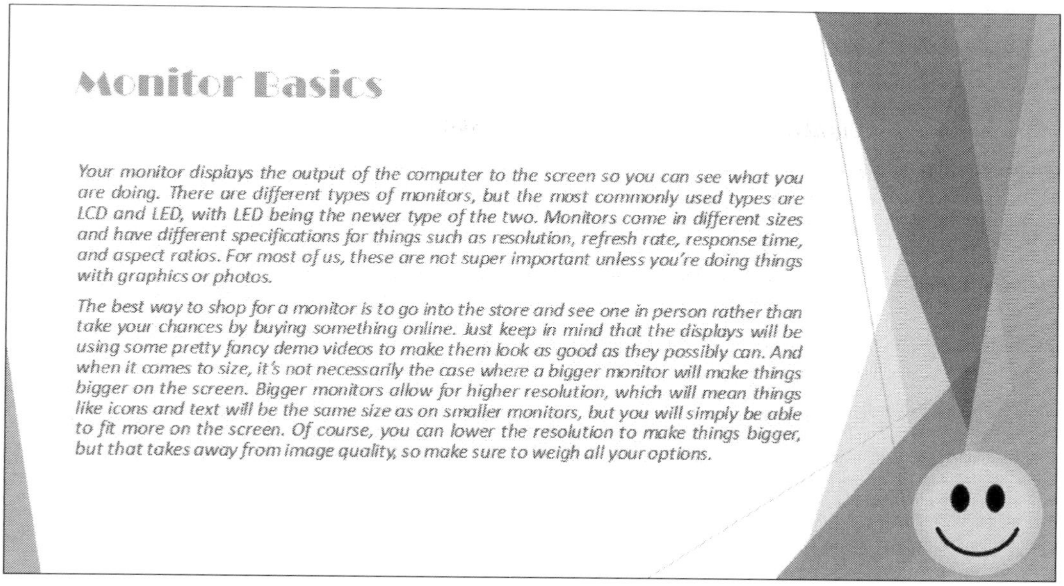

Figure 8.5

If you want your graphics to print out nicely and with all the effects such as shadows etc. then you can choose the *High Quality* option. Just be aware that it will most likely use up more of your ink to make your printouts look their best.

The *Collated* option can be adjusted to control how the pages come out of the printer in regards to their order and the *Color* option can be used to print out your presentation in color, black & white or greyscale.

Finally, the *Edit Header & Footer* link on the bottom will bring you back to the Header and Footer dialog box which we saw back in Chapter 5 and allow you to edit, add or remove any headers and footers you have created.

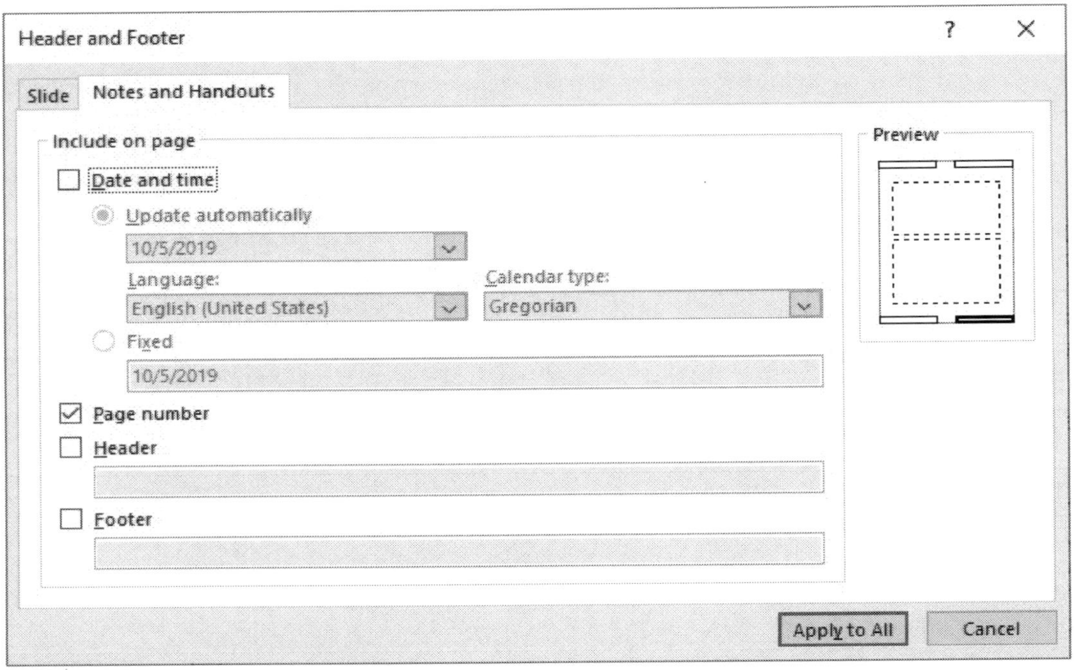

Figure 8.6

When printing always be sure to look at all your pages in the Print Preview and scroll down using the scroll bar or the number selection box at the bottom of the screen before risking wasting time (and ink) on a print job that might not come out the way you want it to.

What's Next?

Now that you have read through this book and taken your PowerPoint skills to the next level, you might be wondering what you should do next. Well, that depends on where you want to go. Are you happy with what you have learned, or do you want to further your knowledge of PowerPoint and become a PowerPoint expert?

If you do want to expand your knowledge, then you can look for some more advanced books on PowerPoint, if that's the path you choose to follow. Focus on mastering the basics, and then apply what you have learned when going to more advanced material.

There are many great video resources as well, such as Pluralsight or CBT Nuggets, which offer online subscriptions to training videos of every type imaginable. YouTube is also a great source for instructional videos if you know what to search for.

If you are content in being a proficient PowerPoint user that knows more than your friends and coworkers, then just keep on practicing what you have learned. Don't be afraid to poke around with some of the settings and tools that you normally don't use and see if you can figure out what they do without having to research it since learning by doing is the most effective method to gain new skills.

Thanks for reading **PowerPoint Made Easy**. You can also check out the other books in the Made Easy series for additional computer related information and training. You can get more information on my other books on my Computers Made Easy Book Series website.

https://www.madeeasybookseries.com/

You should also check out my computer tips website, as well as follow it on Facebook to find more information on all kinds of computer topics.

www.onlinecomputertips.com
https://www.facebook.com/OnlineComputerTips/

About the Author

James Bernstein has been working with various companies in the IT field since 2000, managing technologies such as SAN and NAS storage, VMware, backups, Windows Servers, Active Directory, DNS, DHCP, Networking, Microsoft Office, Photoshop, Premiere, Exchange, and more.

He has obtained certifications from Microsoft, VMware, CompTIA, ShoreTel, and SNIA, and continues to strive to learn new technologies to further his knowledge on a variety of subjects.

He is also the founder of the website onlinecomputertips.com, which offers its readers valuable information on topics such as Windows, networking, hardware, software, and troubleshooting. James writes much of the content himself and adds new content on a regular basis. The site was started in 2005 and is still going strong today.

Printed in Great Britain
by Amazon

68946302R00095